MENSA
ALL-COLOR
PUZZLE
BOOK

A FIREFLY BOOKS

Published by Firefly Books Ltd., 2000

Text and puzzle content copyright © 2000 British Mensa Limited
Design and artwork copyright © 2000 Carlton Books Limited

First Printing

U.S. Cataloging-in-Publication Data

Allen, Robert.
    Mensa all-color puzzle book 2 / Robert Allen. –1st ed.
[256]p.: col. ill. ; cm. (2 vol. set)
Summary: Over 450 brain teasers, from easy to hard, all with answers.
ISBN 1-55209-500-2 (v.2) (pbk)
1. Puzzles. 2. Mathematical recreations. 3. Games. I. Title.
793.73 --21   2000   CIP

Canadian Cataloguing in Publication Data

Allen, Robert (Robert P.)
    Mensa all-color puzzle book 2
ISBN 1-55209-500-2 (pbk)
1. Puzzles.   I. Title.
GV1493.A442 2000   793.73   C00-930472-X

First published in the United States in 2000 by
Firefly Books (U.S.) Inc.
P.O. Box 1338, Ellicott Station
Buffalo, New York 14205

First published in Canada in 2000 by
Firefly Books Ltd.
3680 Victoria Park Avenue
Willowdate, Ontario M2H 3K1

Project Editor: Lara Maiklem
Art Director: Paul Oakley
Puzzle Checking: John Paines
Original Puzzles Created by: Robert Allen, John Bremner, Carolyn Skitt
Production: Sarah Corteel

Printed in Spain

MENSA
ALL-COLOR
PUZZLE
BOOK 2

Robert Allen

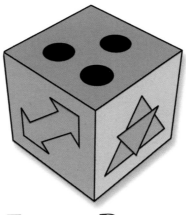

FIREFLY BOOKS

Joining a Mensa society

Mensa Canada and American Mensa are two national branches of the international Mensa society, which includes more than 100,000 people in 80 countries. Members of Mensa have one thing in common: an IQ in the top two percent. Nearly 3,000 Canadians and 45,000 Americans have found out how bright they are and joined Mensa. That leaves millions of people in North America alone who are not Mensa members. You may be one of them.

Looking for mental stimulation?

If you enjoy mental exercise, you'll find lots of good "workout programs" in the magazines published by Mensa Canada and American Mensa. Voice your opinion in one of the newsletters published by local chapters. Learn from the many books and publications that are available to you as a member. Challenge each other at meetings, social events and national gatherings.

Looking for social interaction?

Mensans come from all walks of life, with personalities just as varied. Whatever your interests you will find people with whom you can feel comfortable. Local meetings, parties, get-togethers, lectures, debates, outings and more provide opportunities to exchange ideas and forge new friendships.

Looking for others who share your special interest?

Many Mensa societies include SIGs — special interest groups in which members can enjoy the company of like-minded people, whether your interest is as common as crossword puzzles, as esoteric as Egyptology or as off-the-wall as Monty Python. Some societies have as many as 250 SIGs.

Mensa is about intelligence not education. Take the challenge and discover how smart you really are. You might be surprised. For information or to join, contact your national Mensa society below.

Mensa Canada
329 March Road
Box 11
Kanata, Ontario K2K 2E1
Telephone (613) 599-5897
Fax (613) 599-5897
Email<mensa@igs.net>
WWW<http://www.canada.mensa.org>

American Mensa
1229 Corporate Drive West
Arlington, Texas 76006-6103
Telephone (817) 607-0060
Toll-Free Telephone 1-800-66MENSA
Fax (817) 649-5232
WWW<http://www.us.mensa.org>

Contents

Introduction

The folks at Mensa are always on the lookout for a way to make life just that bit more difficult for you. Don't get the wrong idea, there is definitely no malice involved here, just a persistent desire to make their puzzles as challenging as humanly possible. Recently there was a sudden flash of inspiration and a voice from above called out, "Why not add color?" Color? Surely that will only make the book look prettier? Then the penny dropped (even Very Intelligent People can be a bit thick sometimes), and they realized that color could be used as an integral part of a puzzle. What an idea! With a little bit of ingenuity color can represent letters or numbers in a whole range of intriguing and entertainingly mystifying ways. A whole new vista of puzzling pleasure opened before their eyes.

Take, for example, the Three Triangles puzzle in which numbers are placed at the points of the triangles and the reader has to work out what they signify and then supply the one number that has been left out. It's an old faithful that, even in its simplest form, is capable of endless complication. Now, suppose you color the sides of the triangle? Then you add colored panels inside, and the colors all represent numbers that bear a simple relationship to each other. In a trice the puzzle is transformed to a cunning conundrum that will take hours of nail-biting pleasure to unravel. Oh yes, when it comes to really making your brain ache, you can depend on Mensa!

Easy

Puzzles

PUZZLE 1

Move from square to adjoining square, including diagonals, to discover the longest possible country name from these letters.

Answer see page **88**

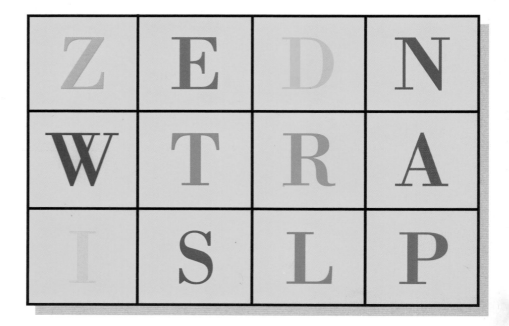

PUZZLE 2

What time should the fourth clock show?

Answer see page **88**

PUZZLE 3

All these children's ages relate to their names. Can you work out how old Andrew is?

Answer see page **88**

PUZZLE 4

Which two boxes in this diagram are similar?

Answer see page **88**

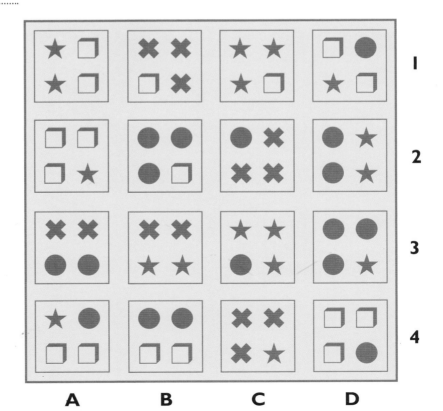

PUZZLE 5

Which of the numbers in each line is the
odd one out?

Answer see page **88**

A 6 12 18 26 30 36

B 135 246 357 468 689

PUZZLE 6

Start at the far left circle and move – to the
right only – along the lines to the far right
circle, collecting the numbers and the ovals
as you go. An oval is worth –37. How
many routes give 152?

Answer see page **88**

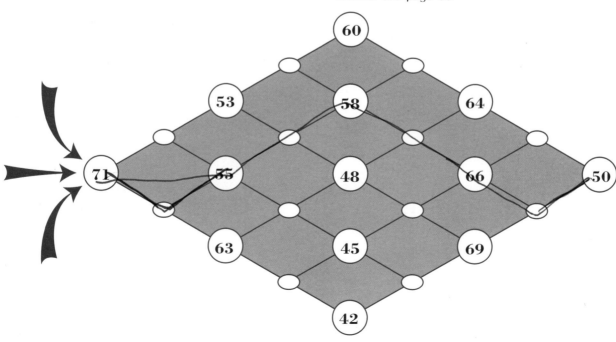

PUZZLE 7

Arrange the pieces to form a square where the numbers read the same horizontally and vertically. What will the finished square look like?

Answer see page **88**

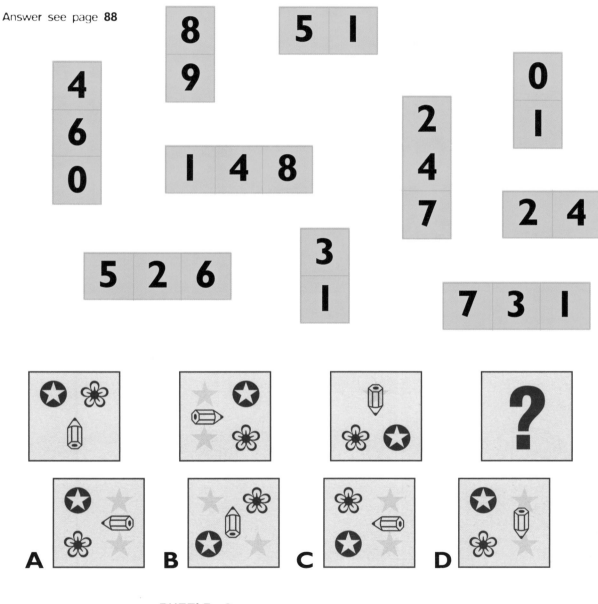

PUZZLE 8

Should A, B, C, or D come next in this series?

Answer see page **88**

13

PUZZLE 9

Four of these animals have something in common. Which is the odd one out? (Clue: think diets.)

Answer see page **88**

PUZZLE 10

What number should replace the question mark?

Answer see page **88**

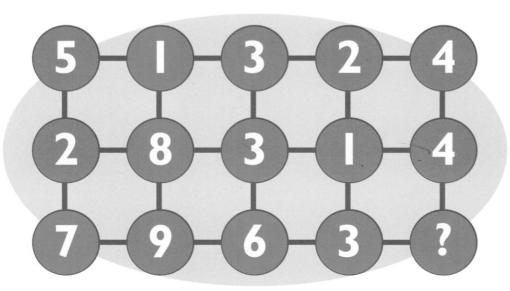

PUZZLE 11

Remove eight of these straight lines to leave only two squares. How can this be done?

Answer see page **88**

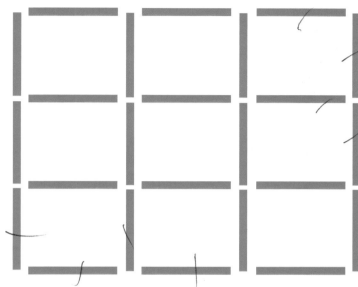

PUZZLE 12

Above is the code for SUMMER HOLIDAYS.
What is written on each line below?

Answer see page **88**

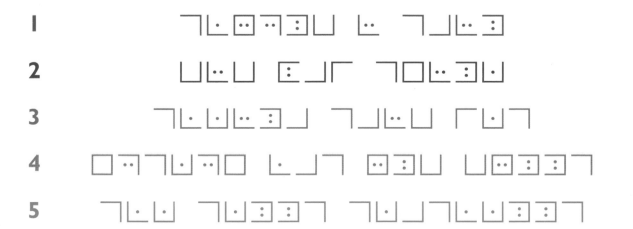

PUZZLE 13

Each shape in the diagram has a value. Work out the values to discover what number should replace the question mark.

Answer see page **88**

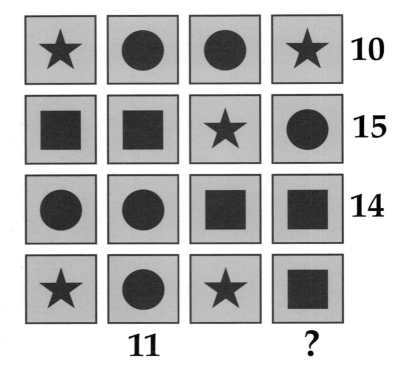

10
15
14
11
?

PUZZLE 14

Which one of the following numbers is the odd one out?

Answer see page **88**

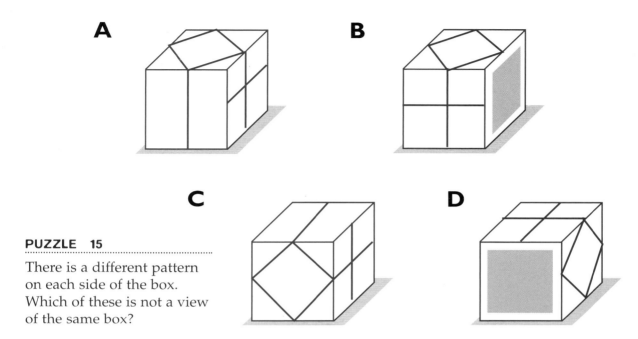

PUZZLE 15

There is a different pattern on each side of the box. Which of these is not a view of the same box?

Answer see page **88**

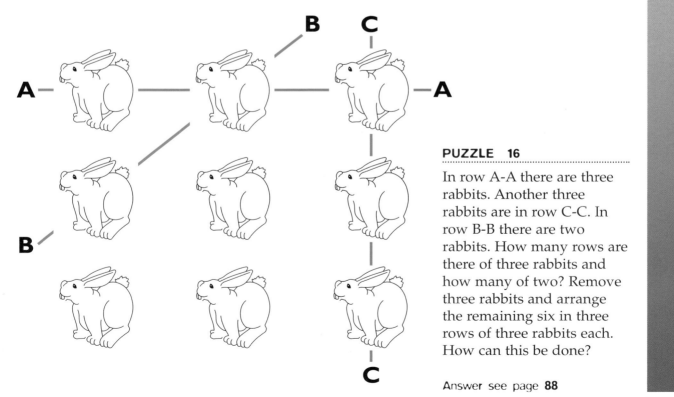

PUZZLE 16

In row A-A there are three rabbits. Another three rabbits are in row C-C. In row B-B there are two rabbits. How many rows are there of three rabbits and how many of two? Remove three rabbits and arrange the remaining six in three rows of three rabbits each. How can this be done?

Answer see page **88**

PUZZLE 17

What time should the fourth clock show?

Answer see page **88**

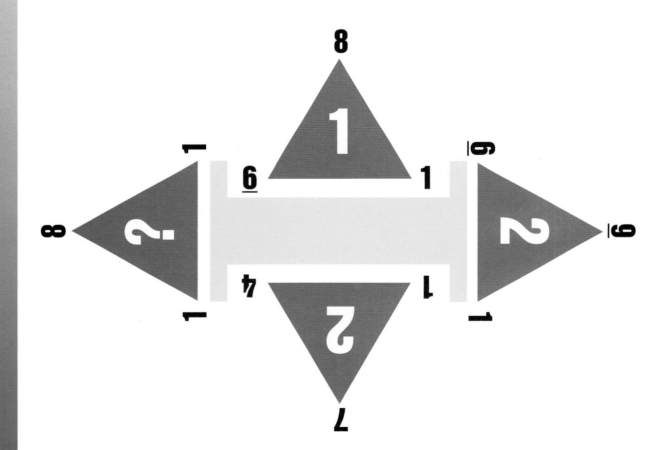

PUZZLE 18

What number should replace the question mark in the fourth triangle?

Answer see page **88**

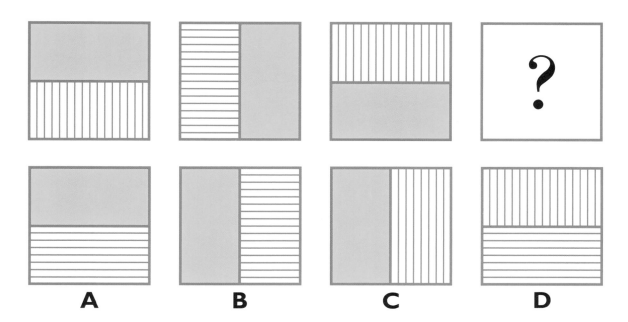

A   **B**   **C**   **D**

PUZZLE 19

Should box A, B, C or D come next in this
series?

Answer see page **89**

PUZZLE 20

What is missing from these series?

Answer see page **89**

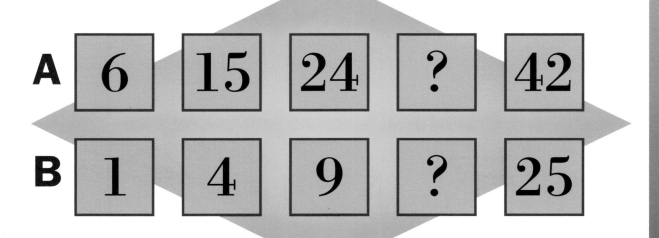

PUZZLE 21

Can you find the 20 creatures in the wordsearch below?

Answer see page **89**

A	B	K	A	Y	N	E	H
R	E	G	I	T	T	P	A
L	A	K	N	B	O	A	M
I	R	A	T	U	O	M	S
O	H	E	K	I	T	O	T
N	S	N	G	A	G	L	E
P	I	G	O	D	E	E	R
M	F	G	A	M	A	L	L
E	S	O	O	M	V	B	E

Ape ✓	Deer ✓	Goat ✓	Llama ✓	Pig ✓
Badger ✓	Dog ✓	Hamster ✓	Mink ✓	Rat ✓
Bear ✓	Fish ✓	Hen ✓	Mole ✓	Tiger ✓
Boa ✓	Gnu ✓	Lion ✓	Moose ✓	Yak ✓

PUZZLE 22

Which of these is not a view of the same three sides of a box?

Answer see page **89**

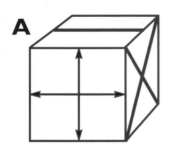

A

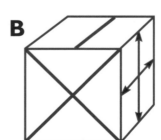

B

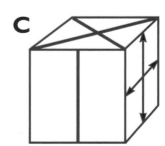

C

PUZZLE 23

Which of the numbers on these balloons is the odd one out?

Answer see page **89**

A

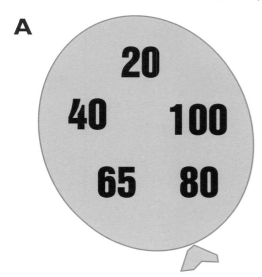

B

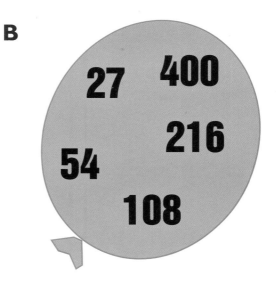

PUZZLE 24

Which two boxes are similar?

Answer see page **89**

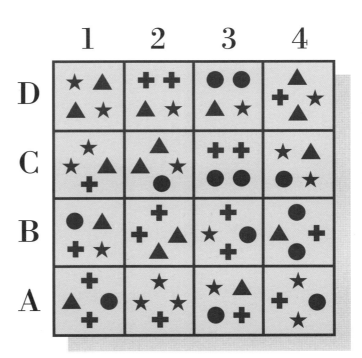

PUZZLE 25

There is only one way to open this safe. You must press each button once only, in the correct order, to reach OPEN. Each button is marked with a direction, U for up, L for left, D for down, R for right. The number of spaces to move is also marked on each button. Which button must you press first to open the safe?

Answer see page **89**

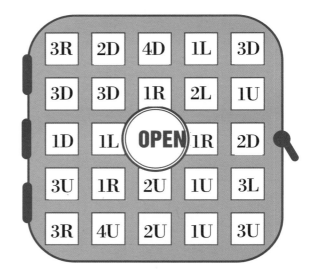

3R	2D	4D	1L	3D
3D	3D	1R	2L	1U
1D	1L	OPEN	1R	2D
3U	1R	2U	1U	3L
3R	4U	2U	1U	3U

Edinburgh 50
Cardiff 30
Bristol 20
Aberdeen ?
Ipswich 90

PUZZLE 26

On this strange signpost how far should it be to Aberdeen?

Answer see page **89**

PUZZLE 27

Replace the vowels in each of the following to form words. Which words are the odd ones out?

Answer see page **89**

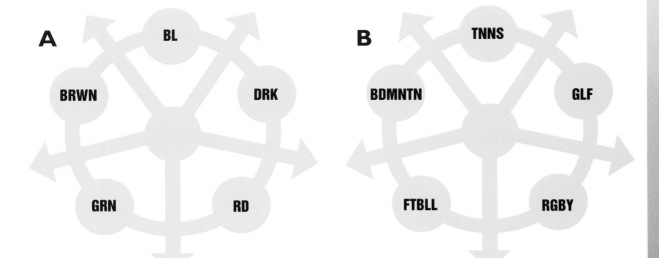

A
BL
BRWN
DRK
GRN
RD

B
TNNS
BDMNTN
GLF
FTBLL
RGBY

PUZZLE 28

What number should replace the question mark?

Answer see page **89**

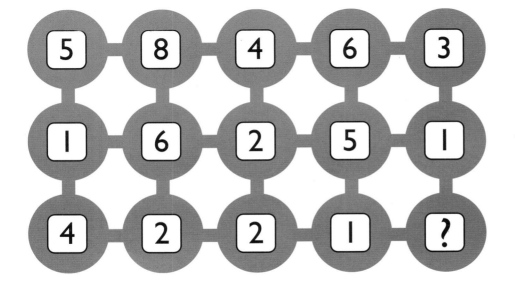

5 8 4 6 3
1 6 2 5 1
4 2 2 1 ?

PUZZLE 29

Match each of the words shown with one of the colors. Each pair will make a well-known expression.

Answer see page **89**

SNOW

JET

BLOOD

EMERALD

MIDNIGHT

HOUSE

GIN

JUICE

PROSE

BOARD

CHEESE

PUZZLE 30

Match each of the colors shown with one of the words from the list. Each pair will comprise a well-known expression.

Answer see page **89**

PUZZLE 31

What color continues this series?

Answer see page **89**

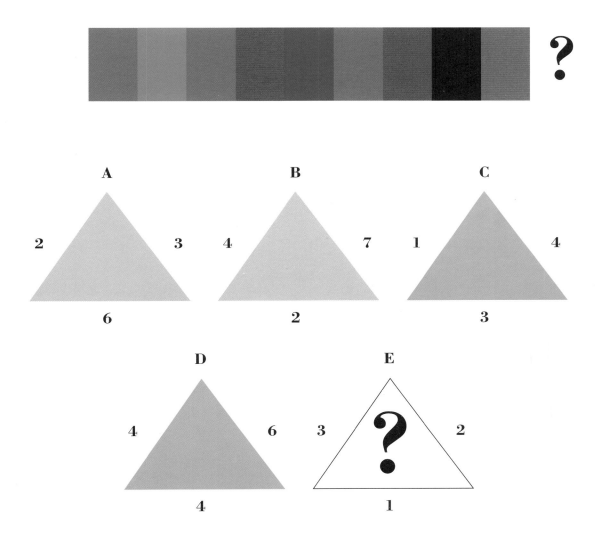

PUZZLE 32

What color should E be?

Answer see page **89**

PUZZLE 33

Each shape in this diagram has a value. Work out the values to discover what numbers should replace the question marks.

Answer see page **89**

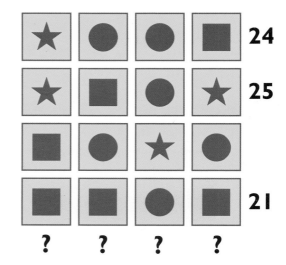

PUZZLE 34

Which route should the bear take to get to the woods?

Answer see page **89**

26

PUZZLE 35

Which of these discs is the odd one out?

Answer see page **89**

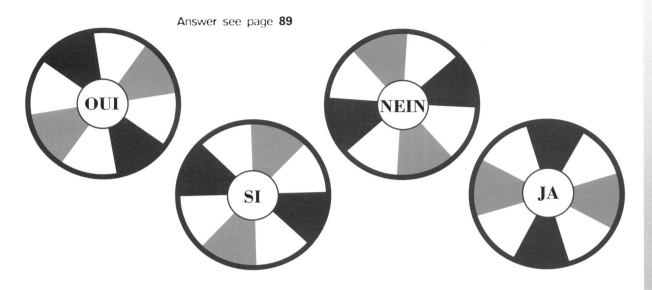

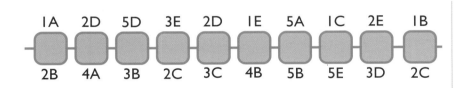

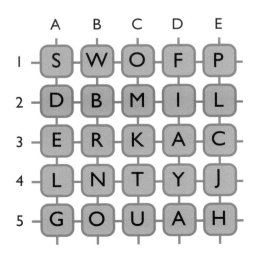

PUZZLE 36

The wordframe, when filled with the correct letters will give the name of a city in England and Alabama. The letters are arranged in the coded square. There are two possible letters to fill each square of the wordframe, one correct, one incorrect.

Answer see page **89**

PUZZLE 37

Which of the following numbers is the odd one out?

Answer see page **90**

A

313 454 262 695 727

B

4 8 10 32 64 128

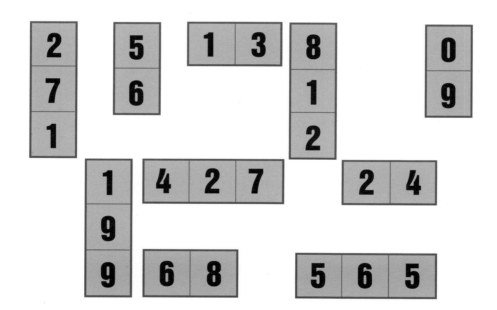

PUZZLE 38

Arrange the pieces to form a square where the numbers read the same horizontally and vertically

.Answer see page **90**

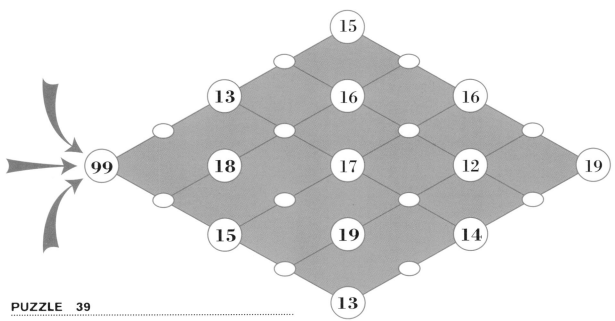

PUZZLE 39

Start at the far left circle and move, to the right only, along the lines to the far right circle, collecting numbers and ovals as you go. Each oval has a value of –41. How many routes give 0?

Answer see page **90**

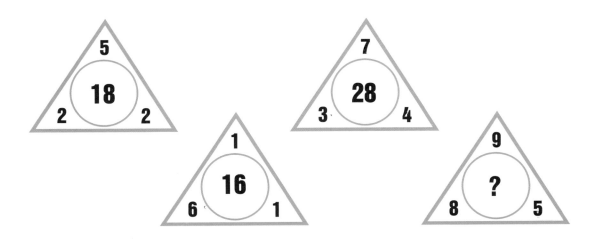

PUZZLE 40

What number should replace the question mark?

Answer see page **90**

PUZZLE 41

Here is an unusual safe. Each button must be pressed once only, in the correct order, to reach OPEN. The direction to move, i for in, o for out, c for clockwise, and a for counterclockwise is marked on each button. The number of spaces to move is also shown on each button. Which button is the first you must press to open the safe?

Answer see page **90**

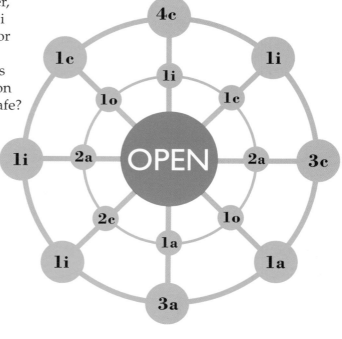

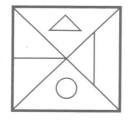 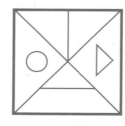  

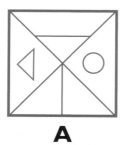 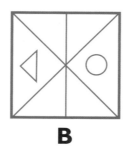 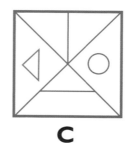 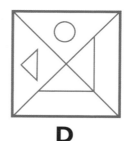

A   **B**   **C**   **D**

PUZZLE 42

Should A, B, C or D come next in the series?

Answer see page **90**

1 **2** **3** **4**

PUZZLE 43

What time should the fourth clock show?

Answer see page **90**

PUZZLE 44

Choose the odd one out on each line and write its initial in the space alongside. When completed these initials will give a word reading downwards. What is the word?

Answer see page **90**

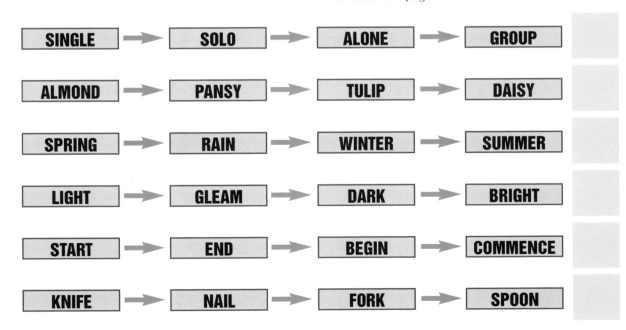

SINGLE →	SOLO →	ALONE →	GROUP
ALMOND →	PANSY →	TULIP →	DAISY
SPRING →	RAIN →	WINTER →	SUMMER
LIGHT →	GLEAM →	DARK →	BRIGHT
START →	END →	BEGIN →	COMMENCE
KNIFE →	NAIL →	FORK →	SPOON

PUZZLE 45

Move from square to adjoining square –
including diagonals – to discover the
longest possible word from these letters.

Answer see page **90**

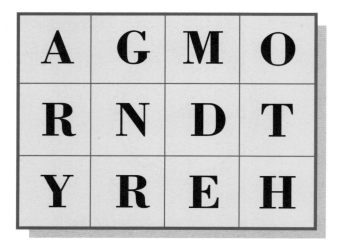

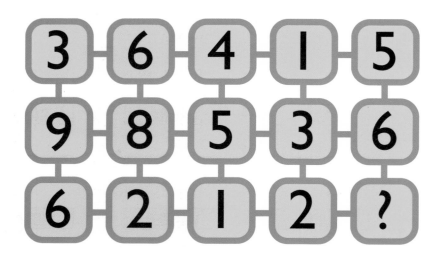

PUZZLE 46

What number should replace the question
mark?

Answer see page **90**

PUZZLE 47

Which two boxes in this diagram are similar?

Answer see page **90**

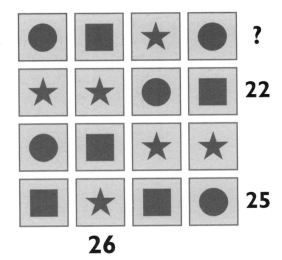

PUZZLE 48

Each shape in this diagram has a value.
Work out the values to discover what
number should replace the question mark.

Answer see page **90**

PUZZLE 49

The fares for these train rides all relate to the place names in England. What is the fare to Oxford ?

Answer see page **90**

Bath £17
Brighton £34
London £24
Taunton £26
Oxford ?

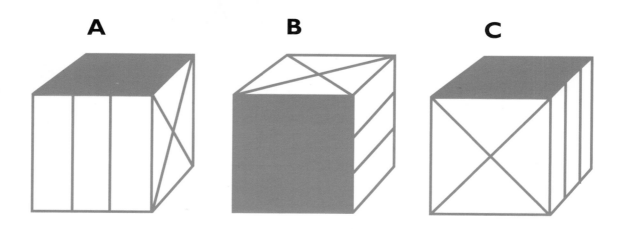

A   **B**   **C**

PUZZLE 50

Which of the above is not a view of the same three sides of a box?

Answer see page **90**

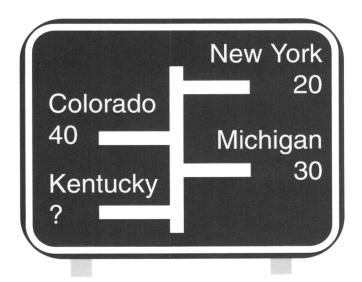

PUZZLE 51

The distances on this fictitious signpost relate to the states' placenames. How far is it to Kentucky?

Answer see page **90**

PUZZLE 52

These jumbled letters spell the names of two tennis stars. Who are they?

Answer see page **90**

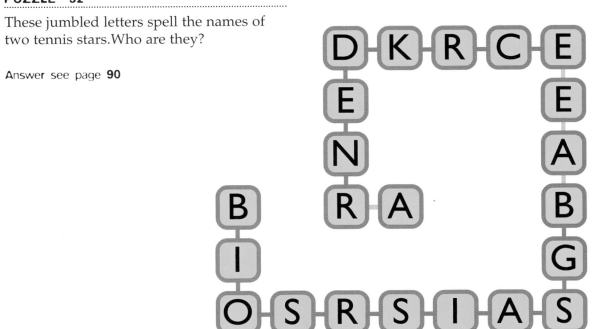

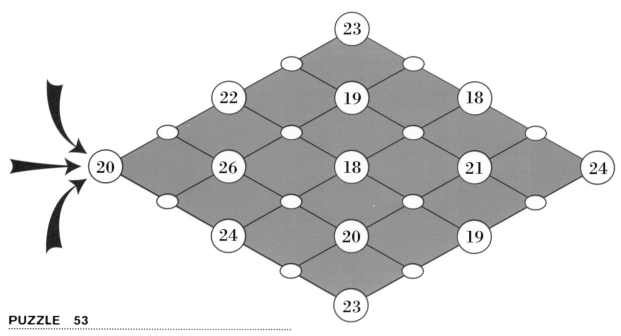

PUZZLE 53

Start at the far left circle and move – to the right only – along the lines to the far right circle, collecting the numbers and the ovals as you go. Each oval has a value of -13. What are the minimum and maximum totals possible?

Answer see page **90**

PUZZLE 54

Which of the boxes continues this sequence and replaces the question mark?

Answer see page **90**

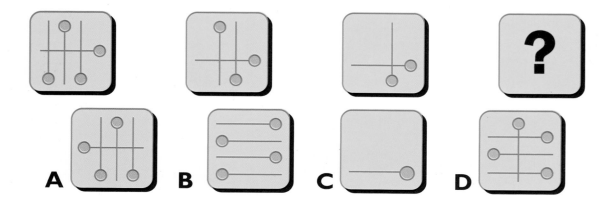

PUZZLE 55

If you go from square to adjoining square – including diagonals – what country will you find using all the letters only once?

Answer see page **90**

A	L	E
N	V	U
E	E	Z

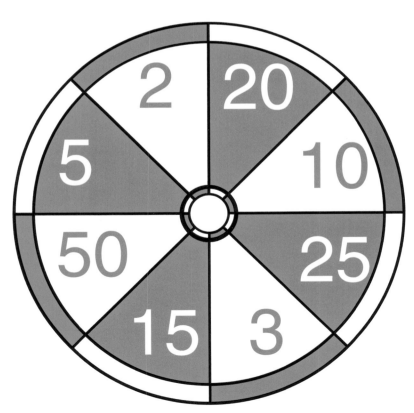

PUZZLE 56

On this unusual dartboard how many different ways are there to score 30 with three darts? Every dart must land in a segment (more than one dart may land in each), and all must score. The same three scores in a different order do not count as another way.

Answer see page **90**

2	1	4	7
5	4	5	9
3	1	8	6
8	3	?	4

PUZZLE 57

What number should replace the question mark?

Answer see page **90**

1   2   3   4

PUZZLE 58

The minute and hour hands move separately on these strange clocks. What time should the fourth clock show?

Answer see page **90**

PUZZLE 59

Should A, B, C or D come next in this series?

Answer see page **90**

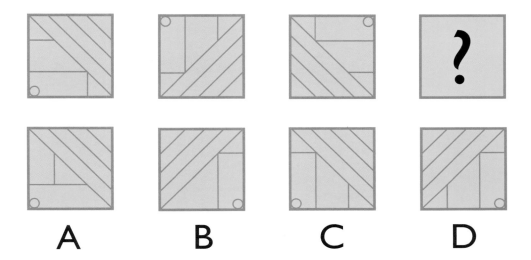

A   B   C   D

PUZZLE 60

Each shape in the diagram has a value. Work out the values to discover what number should replace the question mark.

Answer see page **90**

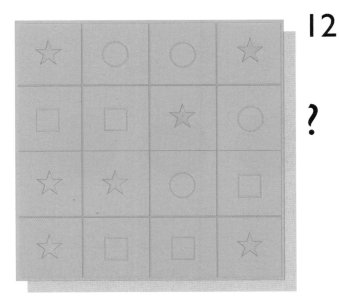

12

?

17 15

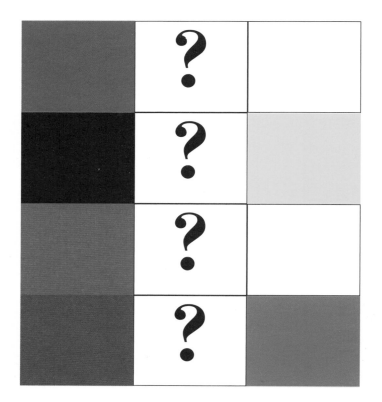

PUZZLE 61

What color could replace the question marks?

Answer see page **90**

PUZZLE 62

Orange is the odd one out. Why?

Answer see page **91**

PUZZLE 63

Does white belong with
group A or B?

Answer see page **91**

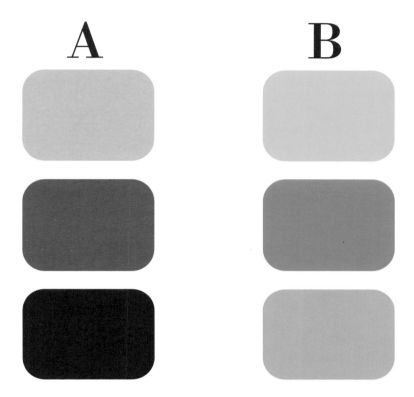

A   B

?

PUZZLE 64

Can you continue this series?

Answer see page **91**

PUZZLE 65

What number should replace the question mark?

Answer see page **91**

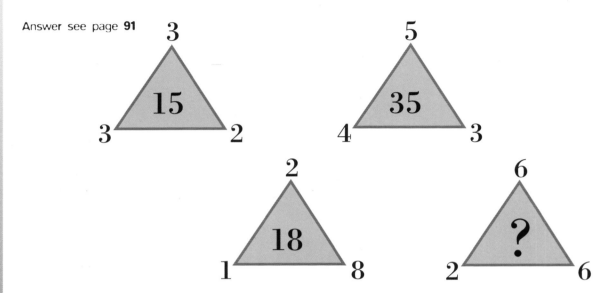

PUZZLE 66

What number is missing from this series?

Answer see page **91**

PUZZLE 67

What numbers should replace the question marks?

Answer see page **91**

8	1	2	4
6	1	3	7
9	1	7	8
5	1	4	9
8	?	?	8

1   2   3   4

PUZZLE 68

What time should the fourth clock show?

Answer see page **91**

PUZZLE 69

Each shape in the diagram has a value. Work out the values to discover what number should replace the question mark.

Answer see page **91**

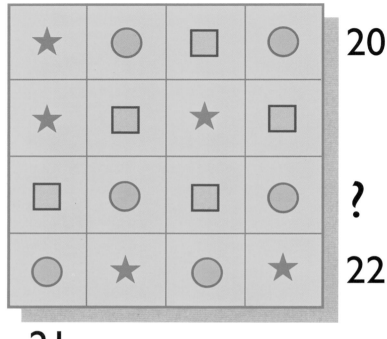

PUZZLE 70

The wordframe below, when filled with the correct letters, will give the name of a composer. The letters are arranged in the coded square. There are two possible letters to fill each square of the wordframe, one correct, the other is incorrect each time. Who is the composer?

Answer see page **91**

	A	B	C	D	E
1	W	T	E	D	E
2	F	C	R	H	P
3	E	U	A	I	U
4	K	M	B	V	S
5	O	L	J	G	N

44

PUZZLE 71

What number should
replace the question mark?

Answer see page **91**

6	2	4
9	4	5
8	7	1
4	1	?

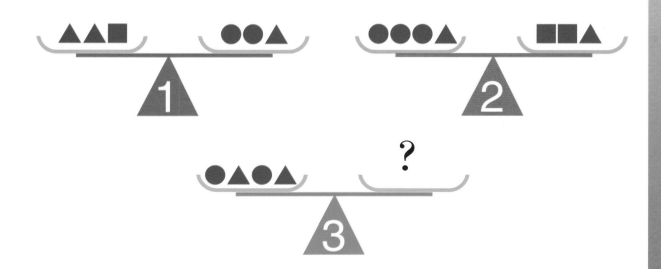

PUZZLE 72

Each shape has a value. Scales 1 and 2 are
in perfect balance. How many squares are
needed to balance scale 3?

Answer see page **91**

PUZZLE 73

Start at the far left circle and move – to the right only – along the lines to the far right circle, collecting numbers and ovals as you go. Each oval has a value of –20. What is the most common score?

Answer see page **91**

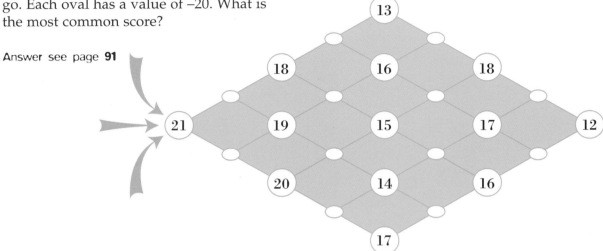

PUZZLE 74

Arrange the pieces to form a square where the numbers read the same horizontally and vertically. What will the finished square look like?

Answer see page **91**

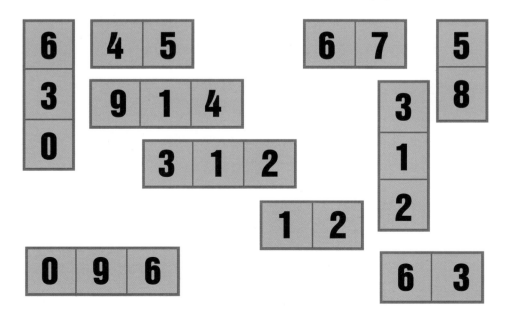

46

PUZZLE 75

Three artists, Michelangelo, Constable and Leonardo Da Vinci are hidden in this coded message.
Who are the five artists below them?

Answer see page **91**

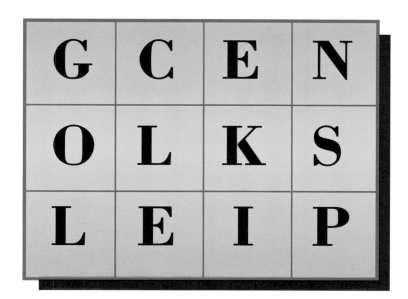

PUZZLE 76

Move from square to adjoining square – including diagonals – and, using all the letters, find a musical instrument.

Answer see page **91**

PUZZLE 77

The hands on these clocks move in a strange but logical way. What is the time on the fourth clock?

Answer see page **91**

A B C D

	A	B	C	D
1	B B A A	A B A C	A A A A	B B A C
2	B B A B	A A A B	C C B B	A C A C
3	C C C C	B A B C	A A C C	B B B C
4	B C C A	A A A C	B B B B	C A C B

PUZZLE 78

Which two boxes contain exactly the same letters? (They may be in a different order.)

Answer see page **91**

PUZZLE 79

This strange signpost shows the distances to motor-racing destinations. How far is it to Hockenheim?

Answer see page **91**

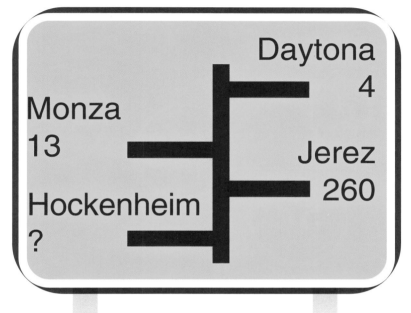

N	B	W	R	Y	A	V	M	D	A
X	E	J	V	D	H	A	O	I	C
H	B	W	A	C	R	K	N	A	F
Y	D	V	M	I	T	R	T	K	G
K	E	F	Z	E	O	W	A	S	N
N	Q	O	X	F	X	Q	N	A	I
B	N	A	I	G	P	I	A	L	M
A	S	L	H	C	B	F	C	A	O
P	A	J	N	O	G	E	R	O	Y
C	O	L	O	R	A	D	O	G	W

PUZZLE 80

In the grid you can find all the American States listed below.

Answer see page **91**

Alaska   California   Montana   New Mexico   Texas
Arizona   Colorado   Nevada   Oregon   Wyoming

PUZZLE 81

In her piggy bank, Jane has $5.24. The sum is made up of an equal number of four coins from 1¢, 5¢, 10¢, 25¢, 50¢ and $1, Which four coins does she have and how many of each of them?

Answer see page **92**

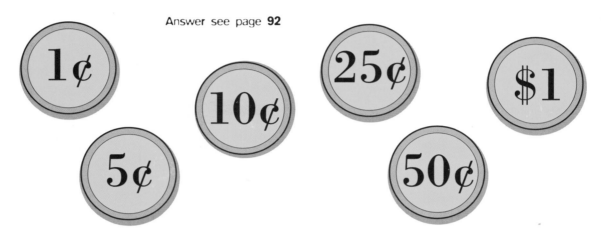

PUZZLE 82

What two digits will replace the question marks?

Answer see page **92**

PUZZLE 83

This grid contains three sports all spelled in the correct order, but mixed with the other two. What are they?

Answer see page **92**

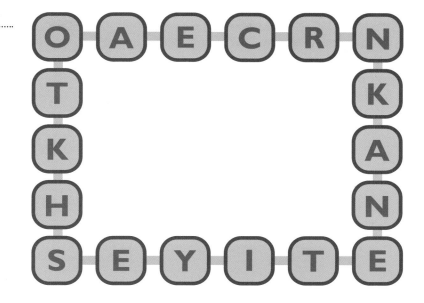

PUZZLE 84

The codes for these letters are shown below. Who are these famous historical scientists?

Answer see page **92**

A
B
C
D
E
F

G
H
I
L
M
N

O
P
R
S
T
U

A
B
C
D
E

F
G
H
I
J

PUZZLE 85

Each same letter in this grid has the same value. What number should replace the question mark and what is the value of each letter?

Answer see page **92**

A	B	B	A	**30**
C	C	A	B	**?**
A	A	B	C	
A	C	C	A	

26   33

PUZZLE 86

Starting from the top left corner, follow the arrows in a continuous down and up route. Which direction, north, south, east or west, should go in the empty space?

Answer see page **92**

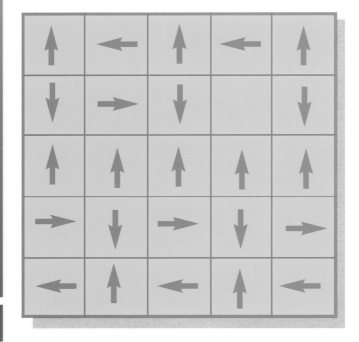

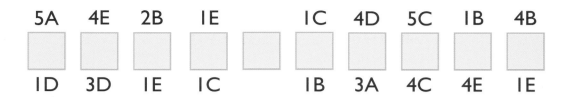

5A	4E	2B	1E		1C	4D	5C	1B	4B
ID	3D	1E	1C		1B	3A	4C	4E	1E

	A	**B**	**C**	**D**	**E**
1	G	R	T	J	E
2	P	K	C	B	W
3	Y	X	F	I	H
4	U	N	Z	A	O
5	M	D	S	V	L

PUZZLE 87

The wordframe above, when filled with the correct letters, gives the name of a famous boxer. However, to make things interesting you have to decide which letters from the grid (right) are correct.

Answer see page **92**

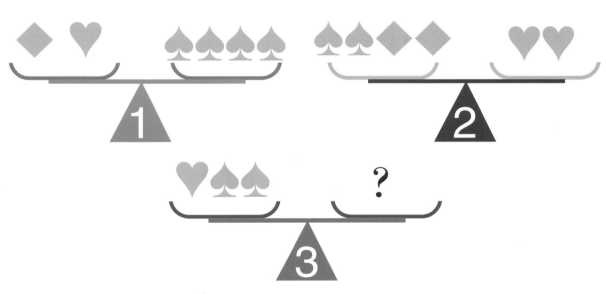

PUZZLE 88

Scales 1 and 2 are in perfect balance.
How many diamonds will balance scale 3?

Answer see page **92**

PUZZLE 89

Which of these is not a view of the same box?

Answer see page **92**

A

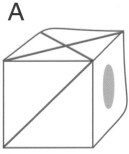

B

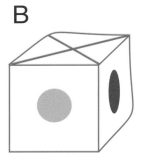

C

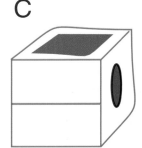

D

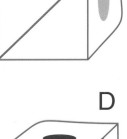

E

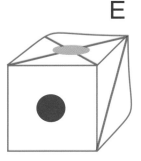

F

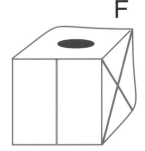

PUZZLE 90

What number should replace the question mark in the bottom sector?

Answer see page **92**

PUZZLE 91

Arrange these pieces to form a square
where the numbers read the same
horizontally and vertically. What will the
finished square look like?

Answer see page **92**

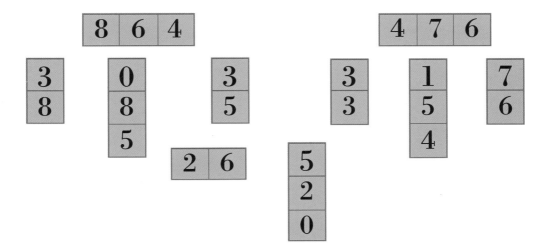

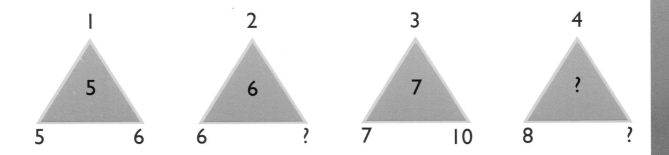

PUZZLE 92

There is a simple logic to the numbers in
and around these triangles. Which
numbers should replace the question
marks?

Answer see page **92**

PUZZLE 93

Can you find a letter to replace the
question mark?

Answer see page **92**

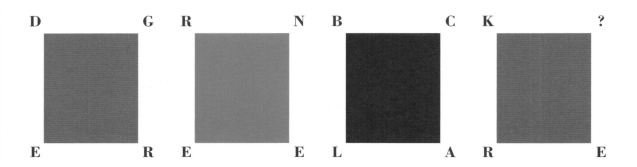

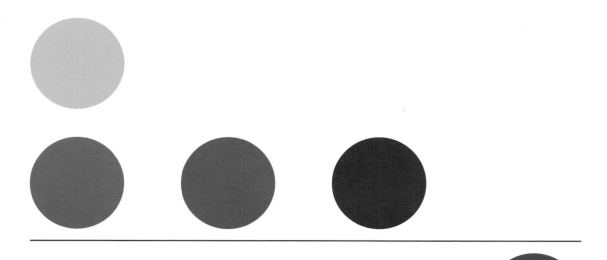

PUZZLE 94

Does pink go above or below the line?

Answer see page **92**

PUZZLE 95

What letter completes the third triangle?

Answer see page **92**

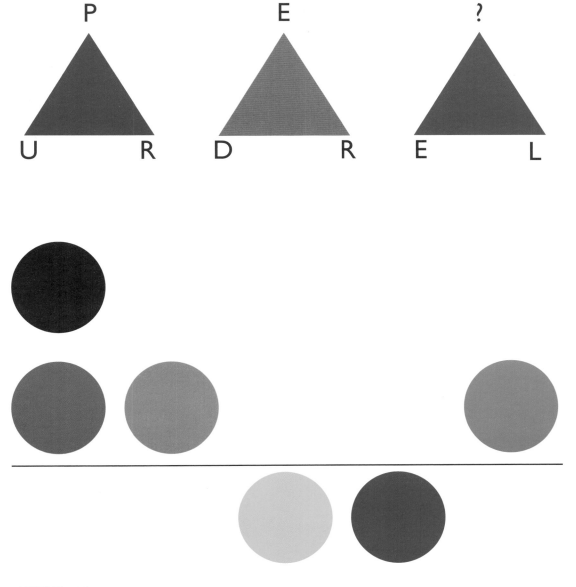

PUZZLE 96

Should black go above or below the line?

Answer see page **92**

PUZZLE 97

This is an unusual safe. To open it you must press the OPEN button, but you must first press all the other buttons in the correct order. This can only be done by following the directions and the number of steps to be taken. Which is the first button you should push?

Answer see page **92**

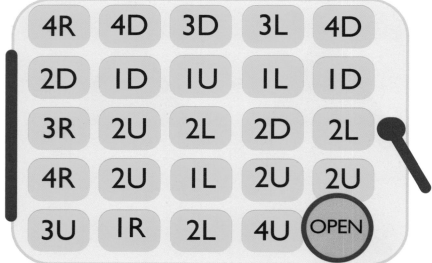

PUZZLE 98

Which box follows the shapes in the first three boxes?

Answer see page **92**

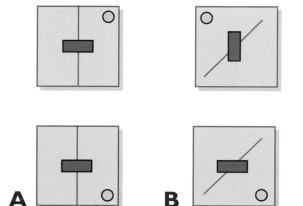

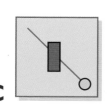

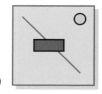

A   B   C   D

PUZZLE 99

The hands on these clocks move in a strange but logical way. What is the time on the fourth clock?

Answer see page **93**

FINISH

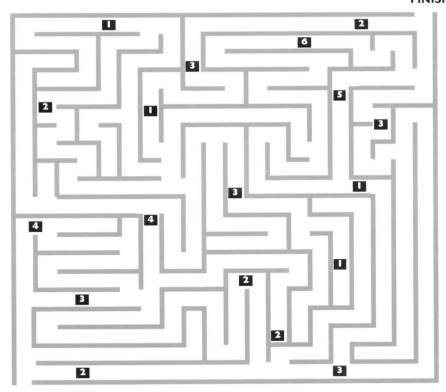

START

PUZZLE 100

This is an unusual maze. There are a few ways of completing it, but the aim is to collect as few points as possible. What is the lowest possible score?

Answer see page **93**

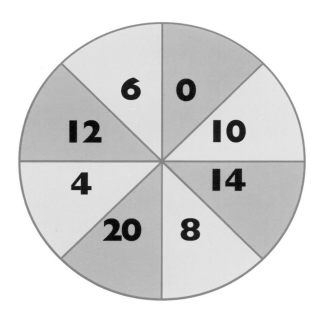

PUZZLE 101

You have three darts to throw at this dartboard. All must land in a segment to score – even 0 – and none can miss. Although more than one dart can land in the same segment, only one order for each set of three can count. How many different ways are there to score 32?

Answer see page **93**

PUZZLE 102

Madonna's fan club has 1500 members, Mariah Carey's fan club is 1101 strong and there are 1201 Metallica fans. How many members are there in Michael Jackson's fan club?

Answer see page **93**

PUZZLE 103

What numbers replace the question marks?

Answer see page **93**

4	7	4	9	5
8	5	1	3	6
3	7	6	?	?

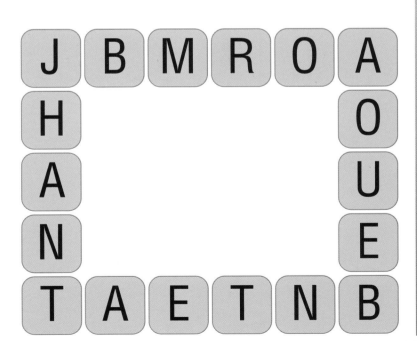

PUZZLE 104

The names of one former baseball star and one former football star have been hidden in this frame. Who are they?

Answer see page **93**

PUZZLE 105

Each same symbol has the same value in this grid. What number replaces the question mark and what are the symbols' values?

Answer see page **93**

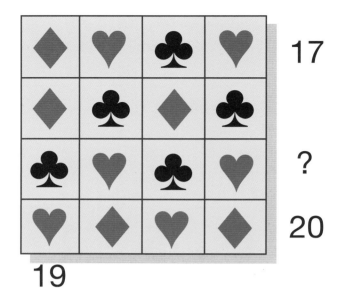

17

?

20

19

A

midnight

B

a.m.

PUZZLE 106

This clock was correct at midnight (A), but lost one minute per hour from that moment on. It stopped one hour ago (B), having run for less than 24 hours. What is the time now?

Answer see page **93**

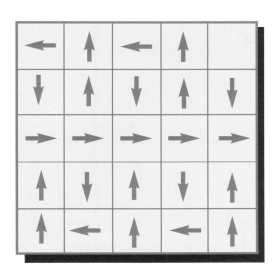

PUZZLE 107

Starting at the top left corner, the arrows in this grid form a logical sequence. What is that sequence and in which direction should the arrow in the empty box point?

Answer see page **93**

PUZZLE 108

Scales 1 and 2 are in perfect balance. How many stars are required to balance scale 3?

Answer see page **93**

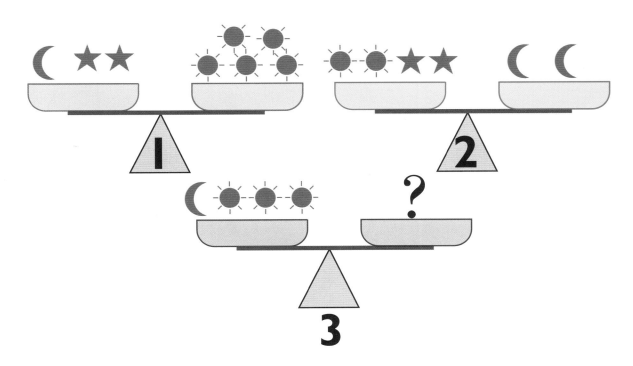

PUZZLE 109

Which of these is not a view of the same box?

Answer see page **93**

A

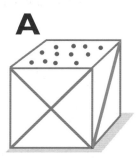

B

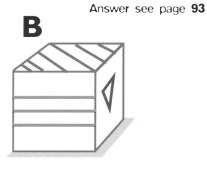

C

D

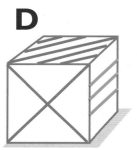

E

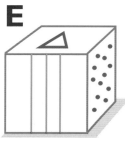

F

PUZZLE 110

What number should replace the question mark?

Answer see page **93**

PUZZLE 111

The hands on these clocks move in a strange but logical way. What time should replace the question mark?

Answer see page **93**

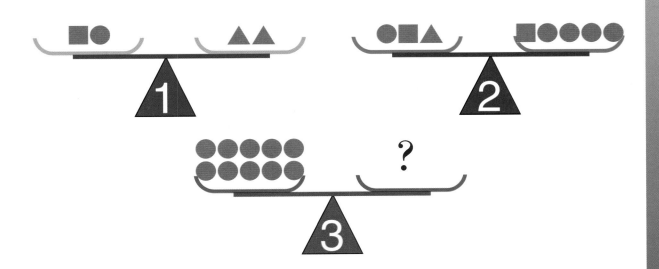

PUZZLE 112

Each shape has a value. Scales 1 and 2 are in perfect balance. How many squares are needed to balance scale 3?

Answer see page **93**

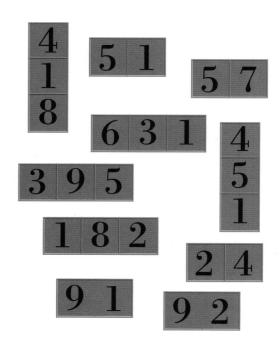

PUZZLE 113

Arrange the pieces to form a square where the numbers read the same vertically and horizontally. What will the finished square look like?

Answer see page **93**

PUZZLE 114

Each shape in the diagram has a value. Work out the values to discover what number should replace the question mark.

Answer see page **93**

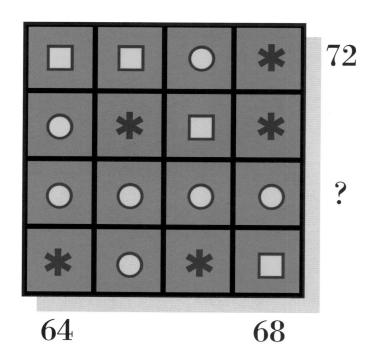

PUZZLE 115

Each shape has a value. Scales 1 and 2 are
in perfect balance. How many squares are
needed to balance scale 3?

Answer see page **93**

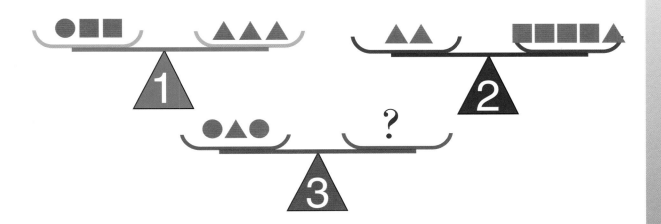

PUZZLE 116

The minute and hour hands are moving
separately on these weird clocks. What
time will the fourth clock show?

Answer see page **93**

PUZZLE 117

Start at the far left circle and move along the lines to the far right circle, collecting the numbers, the diamonds and the ovals as you go. Each oval has a value of -10. Each diamond has a value of -15. What are the minimum and maximum totals possible?

Answer see page **93**

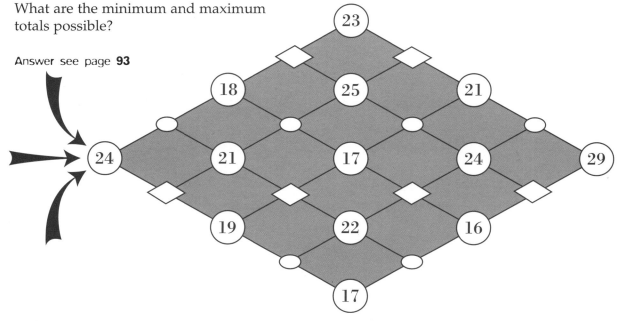

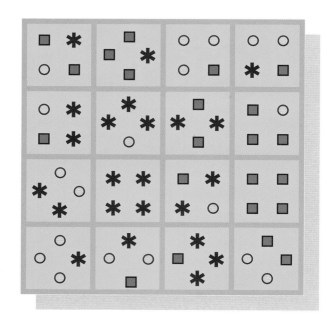

PUZZLE 118

Which two boxes in the diagram are similar?

Answer see page **93**

PUZZLE 119

What number should
replace the question mark?

Answer see page **93**

3	1	4	2	7
5	6	6	5	0
7	8	9	6	9
1	9	4	1	5
2	6	?	2	5

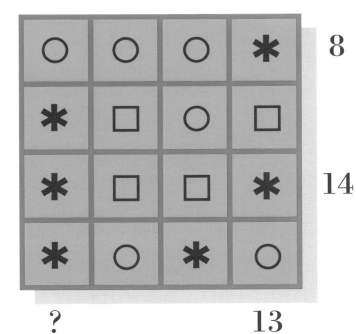

8

14

?   13

PUZZLE 120

Each shape in the diagram
has a value. Work out the
values to discover what
number should replace the
question mark.

Answer see page **93**

PUZZLE 121

Should A, B, C or D come next in this series?

Answer see page **93**

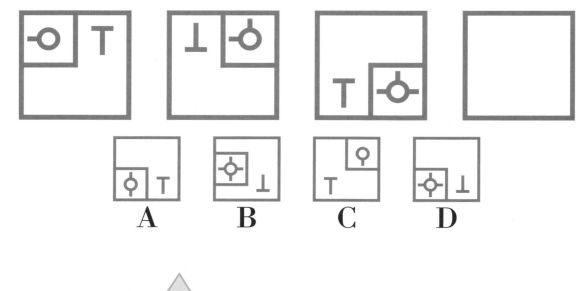

A   B   C   D

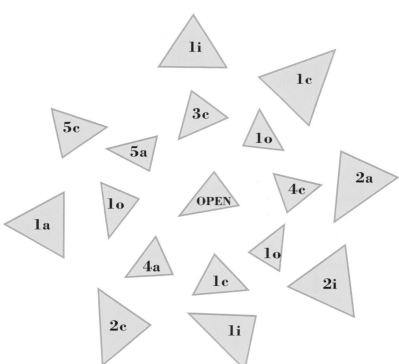

PUZZLE 122

Here is an unusual safe. Each button must be pressed once only, in the correct order, to reach "Open". The direction to move, i for in, o for out, c for clockwise and a for counterclockwise is marked on each button. The number of spaces to move is also shown on each button. Which button is the first you must press?

Answer see page **94**

PUZZLE 123

What number should
replace the question mark?

Answer see page **94**

6	7	4	8
2	3	0	0
4	5	2	4
5	6	3	?

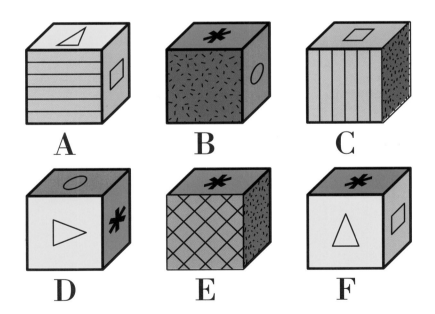

PUZZLE 124

Which of these is not a view of the same
box?

Answer see page **94**

PUZZLE 125

How would you continue the series?

Answer see page **94**

P B R P G

PUZZLE 126

Which of these letters is the odd one out?

Answer see page **94**

PUZZLE 127

Which well-known character is
represented by this rebus?

Answer see page **94**

boy

JUICE

PUZZLE 128

What does this rebus represent?

Answer see page **94**

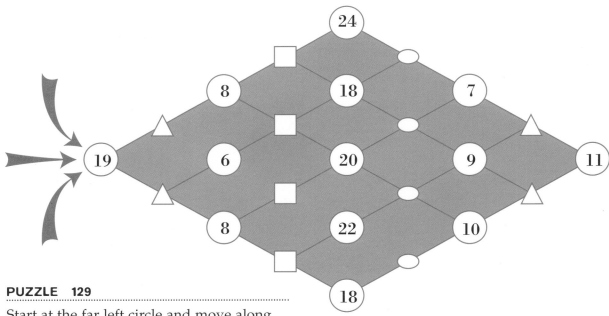

PUZZLE 129

Start at the far left circle and move along the lines to the far right circle, collecting the numbers and shapes as you go. Each oval means divide by 2, each square means multiply by 3, and each triangle means add 13. What are the maximum and minimum totals possible?

Answer see page **94**

PUZZLE 130

Time is moving strangely again on these clocks. What time should the fourth clock show?

Answer see page **94**

PUZZLE 131

What number should be on the bottom line in this diagram?

Answer see page **94**

8	6	5	3	6
5	1	5	2	4
3	5	0	1	2
1	6	5	1	2
?	?	?	?	?

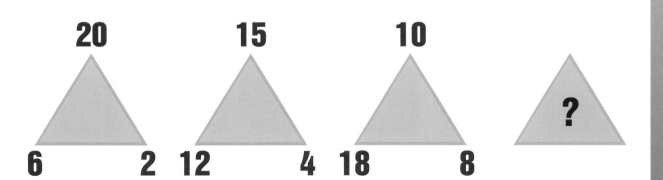

PUZZLE 132

What numbers should surround the fourth triangle?

Answer see page **94**

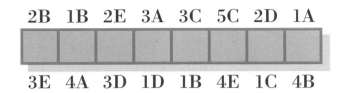

2B	1B	2E	3A	3C	5C	2D	1A

3E 4A 3D 1D 1B 4E 1C 4B

PUZZLE 133

The wordframe above, when filled with the correct letters, will give the name of a Caribbean island. The letters are arranged in the coded square. There are two possible letters to fill each square of the wordframe, one correct, the other incorrect. What is the island?

Answer see page **94**

	A	B	C	D	E
1	H	A	O	B	F
2	V	B	W	T	R
3	E	U	K	M	J
4	U	S	P	A	I
5	G	Z	D	G	X

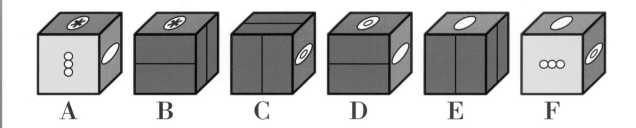

A   B   C   D   E   F

PUZZLE 134

Which of these is not a view of the same box?

Answer see page **94**

PUZZLE 135

There is only one way to open this safe. You must press each button once only, in the correct order, to reach "Open". Each button is marked with a direction, U for up, L for left, R for right, and D for down. The number of spaces to move is also marked on each button. Which is the first button you must press?

Answer see page **94**

4D	4D	1L	3L	OPEN
2R	1D	1U	2L	4L
4R	1L	2D	1U	2L
4R	2R	2L	1D	2U
4R	1U	1U	4U	4U

PUZZLE 136

You have three darts to throw at this strange dartboard. Each dart must score and more than one dart can land in the same segment, but separate scoring rounds may not contain the same three values in a different order. How many different ways are there to score 32?

Answer see page **94**

PUZZLE 137

The distances on this signpost to the Great Lakes have something to do with their names. What is the distance to Lake Superior?

Answer see page **94**

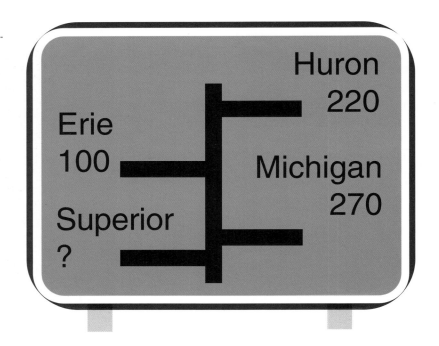

PUZZLE 138

The clocks move in a special way. What time should be on the blank face?

Answer see page **94**

PUZZLE 139

What two numbers should replace the question marks?

Answer see page **94**

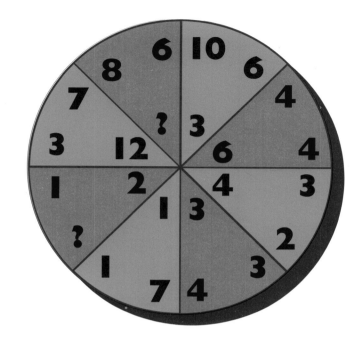

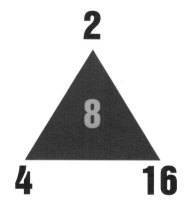

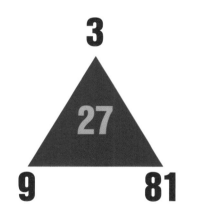

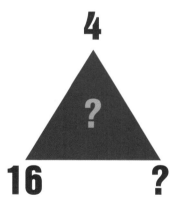

PUZZLE 140

What number can replace the question mark?

Answer see page **94**

PUZZLE 141

Scales 1 and 2 are in perfect balance. How many pairs of cherries will balance scale 3?

Answer see page **94**

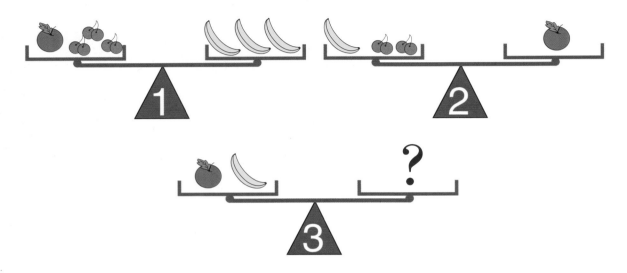

PUZZLE 142

If the semaphore codes below are for Michael Jackson and Paul McCartney, who are the other people shown below?

Answer see page **94**

Michael Jackson =

Paul McCartney =

1

2

3

4

5

PUZZLE 143

Each like symbol in the diagram has the same value – one of which is a negative number. Can you work out the logic and discover what number should replace the question mark and what are the values of the symbols?

Answer see page **94**

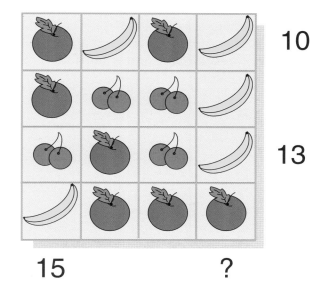

10

13

15   ?

A

midnight

B

p.m.

PUZZLE 144

This clock was correct at midnight (A), but began to lose 3.75 minutes per hour from that moment. It stopped half an hour ago (B), having run for less than 24 hours. What is the correct time now?

Answer see page **94**

PUZZLE 145

This grid of compass directions follows a set pattern in a continuous horizontal line. What direction is missing and what is the order?

Answer see page **95**

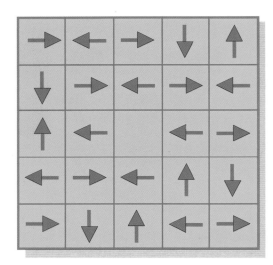

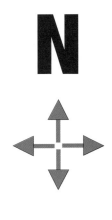

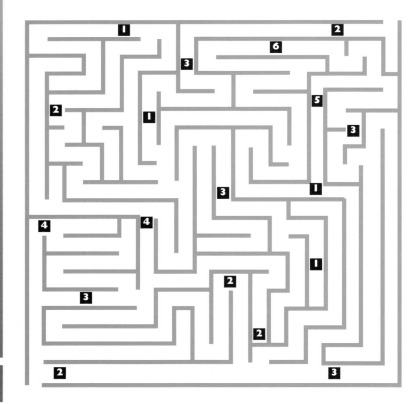

PUZZLE 146

There is more than one way to complete this maze, so the aim is to complete it by collecting as few points as possible. What is the route and how many points are collected?

Answer see page **95**

4SE	1E	4S	1SE	4SW
2S	1E	1NE	1SE	1SW
1E	1NW	OPEN	2NW	2W
3E	3NE	1SW	3NW	1SW
2N	1N	1N	3N	1N

PUZZLE 147

Here is another unusual safe. To reach the OPEN button, all the other buttons must be pressed in the correct order. Each button has a compass direction together with the number of steps needed. Which is the first button you must press?

Answer see page **95**

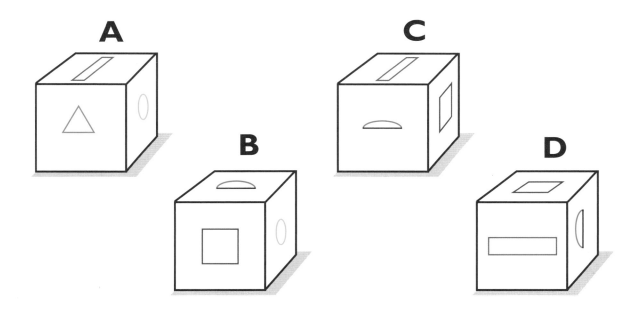

PUZZLE 148

There is a different symbol on each side of the box. Which of these is not a view of the same box?

Answer see page **95**

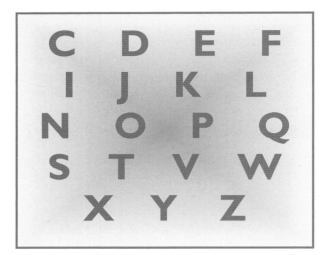

PUZZLE 149

Here is the alphabet with some letters omitted. When you found all the missing ones, they will spell the name of a German city. What is it?

Answer see page **95**

G	X	R	V	F	S	H	P	L	A
D	A	N	U	B	E	Q	F	Z	K
R	P	N	E	N	I	H	R	W	Q
C	Y	F	A	J	N	M	F	J	D
Z	K	E	B	I	E	B	L	E	H
E	B	M	B	U	D	G	E	T	H
R	D	U	S	R	Y	N	Q	V	F
I	Z	E	Q	W	O	J	A	P	X
O	N	P	J	H	T	A	G	U	S
L	Y	G	R	X	V	N	N	B	G

PUZZLE 150

The ten longest rivers in Europe are hidden in this grid. Each is spelled in a straight line with no letters missed nor any gaps, up, down, across or diagonally, forward or backward. Can you find them? They are:

Answer see page **95**

Danube	Meuse
Ebro	Rhine
Elbe	Rhone
Guandiana	Seine
Loire	Tagus

PUZZLE 151

Can you tell how far it is to the Mercedes-Benz garage on this weird signpost?

Answer see page **95**

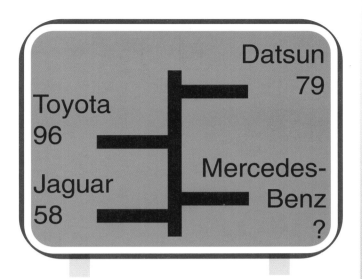

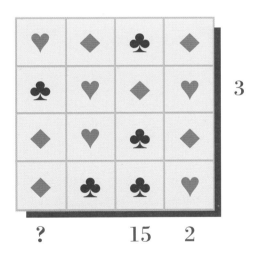

PUZZLE 152

Each same symbol in the diagram has the same value – one of which is a negative number. Can you work out the logic and discover what number should replace the question mark and the values of the symbols?

Answer see page **95**

PUZZLE 155

This clock was correct at midnight (A), but began to lose 10 minutes per hour from that moment. It stopped 2 $\frac{1}{2}$ hours ago

(B), having run for less than 24 hours. What is the correct time now?

Answer see page **95**

midnight

p.m.

PUZZLE 156

The arrows in this grid go in a clockwise spiral starting from the top left corner. In which direction should the missing arrow point?

Answer see page **95**

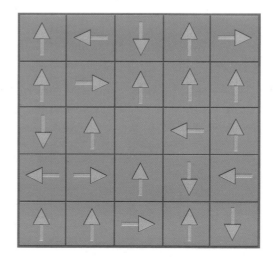

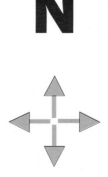

Easy Answers

Answer 1
Switzerland

Answer 2
7:10. The clock moves 15, 20 and 25 minutes forward.

Answer 3
Andrew is 1 year old. The ages relate to the alphabetic position of the first letter of each child's name.

Answer 4
A4 and D1.

Answer 5
A. 26. Multiples of 6 should make it 24.
B. 689. The other numbers' digits increase by one.

Answer 6
4 ways.

Answer 7

2	4	7	3	1
4	6	0	5	1
7	0	1	2	4
3	5	2	6	8
1	1	4	8	9

Answer 8
C.

Answer 9
Elephant. All the others are meat-eating animals.

Answer 10
8. Add the first row to the second row to give the third row.

Answer 11

Answer 12
1. Should I sail
2. Did Ray smile
3. Sheila said yes
4. Museum has old dolls
5. She sells sea shells

Answer 13
13. ★ = 3, ● = 2, ■ = 5.

Answer 14
31. It is the only odd number.

Answer 15
C.

Answer 16
A. 8 rows of three rabbits
B. 28 rows of two rabbits
C. 6 rabbits in three rows of three rabbits can be done like this:

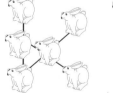 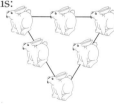

Answer 17
12:30. Each clock moves forward 1 hour and 10 minutes.

Answer 18
6. Subtract the two bottom numbers from the top number to give the middle number.

Answer 19
B.

Answer 20
A. 33. Each number rises by 9.
B. 16. The squares of 1, 2, 3, 4 and 5.

Answer 21

Answer 22
B.

Answer 23
A. 65. The others are all multiples of 20.
B. 400. The other numbers are multiples of 27.

Answer 24
B1 and A3.

Answer 25
3D in column 1 on row 2.

Answer 26
10. The alphabetic position of the first letter multiplied by 10.

Answer 27
A. DRK. The others are all colors, but DRK is dark.
B. BDMNTN. The others are all sports which use a ball. Badminton uses a shuttlecock.

Answer 28
2. Subtract the second row from the top row to give the bottom row.

Answer 29
Snow white, Jet black, Blood red, Emerald green, Midnight blue.

Answer 30
Blue cheese, Blackboard, Purple prose, Orange juice, Pink gin, White House.

Answer 31
Blue. Blue always begins a series of colors beginning with B.

Answer 32
Orange. The numbers are added, an even total produces an orange triangle, an odd one produces pink.

Answer 33
Left to right: 24, 22, 25, 23. ★ = 7, ● = 6, ■ = 5.

Answer 34

Answer 35
Nein. The others are "yes" in European languages. Nein is "no" in German.

Answer 36
Birmingham.

Answer 37
A. 695. The other numbers have the same first and third digits.
B. 10. The numbers double each time and this should be 16.

Answer 38

6	8	1	2	4
8	0	9	5	2
1	9	9	6	7
2	5	6	5	1
4	2	7	1	3

Answer 39
10.

Answer 40
44. Add the three outer numbers together, double them and put the answer in the middle.

Answer 41
1i in the outer circle, between 1i and 1c.

Answer 42
A.

Answer 43
5:05. The clock moves forward 1 hour and 25 minutes each time.

Answer 44
GARDEN. Odd ones out are: Group (others are singles), Almond (others are plants), Rain (others are seasons), Dark (others are light), End (others are start), Nail (others are kitchen implements).

Answer 45
Grandmother.

Answer 46
1. Subtract the top row from the middle row to give the bottom row.

Answer 47
A4 and D1.

Answer 48
21. ★ = 5, ● = 4, ■ = 8.

Answer 49
£24. Consonants are worth £5, vowels are worth £2.

Answer 50
C.

Answer 51
20. Each vowel is worth 10.

Answer 52
Boris Becker and Andre Agassi.

Answer 53
Maximum is 59, minimum is 50.

Answer 54
C.

Answer 55
Venezuela.

Answer 56
4.

Answer 57
2. The outer numbers, when multiplied, give the inner one.

Answer 58
5:20.

Answer 59
D.

Answer 60
20. ★ = 2, ● = 4, ■ = 7

Answer 61
Orange. If you take the initial letters of the colors you get words reading across: BOW, BOY, ROW, BOG.

Answer 62
Orange. It is the only one to start with a vowel.

Answer 63
Group B. All the colors in Group B have an E in them, none of the As do.

Answer 64
No, the number of letters decreases but there is no color with only two letters.

Answer 65
48. Add together the bottom two numbers, multiply the total by the top and place the answer in the middle.

Answer 66
7. It is run of consecutive prime numbers.

Answer 67
1 and 6. On each row, add the two outer numbers to give the middle one.

Answer 68
10:50. The time moves backwards 1 hour, 5 minutes on each clock.

Answer 69
18. ★ = 6, ● = 5, ■ = 4.

Answer 70
Beethoven.

Answer 71
3. In each row, subtract the middle number from the left to give the right.

Answer 72
2 squares.

Answer 73
4 (26 ways).

Answer 74

9	1	4	6	3
1	2	5	3	1
4	5	8	0	2
6	3	0	9	6
3	1	2	6	7

Answer 75
1. Monet
2. Dali
3. Rembrandt
4. Donatello
5. Ernst
6. van Gogh

Answer 76
Glockenspiel.

Answer 77
6:55.

Answer 78
4A and 4D.

Answer 79
104. Multiply the alphabetic position of the first and last letters of each place.

Answer 80

Answer 81
4 each of $1, 25¢, 5¢ and 1¢.

Answer 82
0 and 5. Subtract the lower line from the one immediately above it and put the answer directly below.

Answer 83
Hockey, Karate and Tennis.

Answer 84
A. Galileo
B. Archimedes
C. Oppenheimer
D. Einstein
E. Heisenberg
F. Bell
G. Fleming
H. Ampere
I. Celsius
J. Pascal

Answer 85
29. A = 11, B = 4, C = 7

Answer 86
East.

Answer 87
Mike Tyson.

Answer 88
3 diamonds.

Answer 89
E.

Answer 90
10. The numbers in each sector are added together and the diagonally opposite sectors have the same total.

Answer 91

1	5	4	7	6
5	2	0	3	3
4	0	8	5	8
7	3	5	2	6
6	3	8	6	4

Answer 92
The numbers at the top, middle and left are consecutive. The top and left numbers are then added together to give the right number.

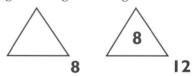

Answer 93
D. The names of the colors are written around the outside of the squares. D is the only letter missing.

Answer 94
Below, all those above have an initial B, those below have P.

Answer 95
P. The letters read RED, PURPLE, with one P missing.

Answer 96
Above. Those above the line have only one syllable, those below have two.

Answer 97
2U on row 4 in column 4.

Answer 98
C. The circle moves 90° counterclockwise, the straight line moves 45° clockwise and the rectangle moves 90° clockwise.

Answer 99
8:05. The clocks move 4 hours and 50 minutes forward each time.

Answer 100
8.

Answer 101
8 ways.

Answer 102
1,251. The values of the Roman numerals in each star's name are added together.

Answer 103
4 and 1. Add the top line to the bottom line to give the middle line.

Answer 104
Babe Ruth and Joe Montana.

Answer 105
14. Diamond = 6, Heart = 4, Club = 3.

Answer 106
6:00 am.

Answer 107
West. The order is West, South, East, North, North, and it runs continuously down column 1, up column 2, down column 3, etc.

Answer 108
4 stars.

Answer 109
F.

Answer 110
10. The three numbers in each sector are added together and the totals in the bottom four segments are double those of their diagonally opposite ones.

Answer 111
2:45. The hour hand moves forward 2 hours each time, the minute hand moves alternately forward 5 minutes and back 10.

Answer 112
2 squares.

Answer 113

4	5	1	9	2
5	6	3	1	4
1	3	9	5	1
9	1	5	7	8
2	4	1	8	2

Answer 114
52. ★ = 17, ● = 13, ■ = 21.

Answer 115
24 squares.

Answer 116
9:15. In each case the hour hand moves forward 1 hour and the minute hand moves 15 minutes forward.

Answer 117
Lowest is 45, highest is 83.

Answer 118
2A and 3C.

Answer 119
1. On each row, subtract the two right numbers from the two left ones. The answer is put in the middle.

Answer 120
16. ★ = 5, ● = 1, ■ = 2.

Answer 121
D. The small square moves clockwise with the circle gaining an extra line each time. The T moves counterclockwise and rotates through 180°.

Answer 122
5a in the inner circle.

Answer 123
6. On each row, 1 is added to the first number to give the second number. Column three has 3 subtracted from column two and column four is double the value of column three.

Answer 124
E.

Answer 125
The number of letters goes 3, 4, 5, 6. Any color with 6 letters would complete the final square.

Answer 126
The yellow P. All the other letters also represent their color.

Answer 127
Little Boy Blue.

Answer 128
Orange juice.

Answer 129
Minimum is 97, maximum is 105.

Answer 130
1:00. In each case, the time is moving back 2 hours 10 minutes.

Answer 131
18500. Each line is deducted from the the line above to give the line below.

Answer 132

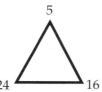

The right number doubles; the left number goes up by 6 and the top number goes down by 5.

Answer 133
Barbados.

Answer 134
E.

Answer 135
1U in row 3 on column 4.

Answer 136
8 ways.

Answer 137
370. Add the alphabetic position of the first and last letters, then multiply by 10.

Answer 138
4:20. The times move forward by 1 hour and 5 minutes, 2 hours and 10 minutes, 4 hours and 20 minutes, and 8 hours and 40 minutes.

Answer 139
Outer 3, inner 9. The numbers in the outer sectors are added together and the sums of the top half are double those of the diagonally opposite bottom halves. The top half numbers in the inner part of the sectors are three times those of the diagonally opposite bottom half ones.

Answer 140
Bottom right = 64, middle = 256.
The left and top numbers are multiplied and the answer is put in the middle. The top and middle numbers are then multiplied and this answer goes to the right.

Answer 141
7 pairs of cherries.

Answer 142
1. Phil Collins.
2. Michael Schumacher.
3. Sean Connery.
4. Mike Tyson.
5. John Lennon.

Answer 143
3. Apples = 6,
Bananas = –1,
Cherries = 4.

Answer 144
8:30 pm.

Answer 145
East. The order is E, W, E, S, N, W.

Answer 146
The lowest possible scoring route is 9.

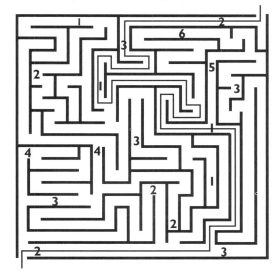

Answer 147
1E on row 2, column 2.

Answer 148
B.

Answer 149
Hamburg.

Answer 150

G	X	R	V	F	$	H	P	L	A
D	A	N	U	B	E	Q	F	Z	K
R	P	N	E	N	I	H	R	W	Q
C	Y	F	A	J	N	M	F	J	D
Z	K	E	B	I	E	B	L	E	H
E	B	M	R	U	D	G	E	T	H
R	D	U	S	R	Y	N	Q	V	F
I	Z	E	Q	W	Q	J	A	P	X
O	N	P	J	H	T	A	G	U	S
L	Y	G	R	X	V	N	N	B	G

Answer 151
119. The alphabetic positions of all the letters of the names are added together.

Answer 152
8. Heart = –2, Diamond = 3, Club = 4.

Answer 153
10:30 pm.

Answer 154
North. The order is N, W, S, N, E, N.

Medium

Puzzles

PUZZLE 155

Can you work out what letter needs to be inserted in the middle to form four dances by combining opposite segments?

Answer see page 140

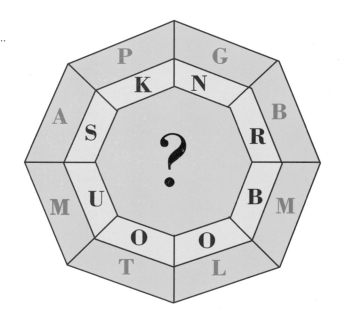

PUZZLE 156

The following names can be found in this grid on either vertical, horizontal or diagonal lines. Can you find them?

Answer see page 140

Raymond Blanc

Paul Bocuse

Robert Carrier

Keith Floyd

Rosamund Grant

Ken Hom

Bruno Loubet

Gary Rhodes

Albert Roux

Anthony Tobin

T	N	A	R	G	D	N	U	M	A	S	O	R
B	Y	N	L	K	L	Q	O	X	C	B	O	A
Q	W	T	F	Z	P	H	K	U	J	B	G	Y
Y	G	H	V	S	N	X	E	O	E	R	C	M
D	V	O	W	E	M	D	I	R	S	U	K	O
J	K	N	K	D	B	P	T	T	U	N	O	N
P	M	Y	S	O	S	C	H	R	C	O	P	D
P	F	T	Y	H	A	Y	F	E	O	L	J	B
Z	W	O	U	R	Z	G	L	B	B	O	C	L
F	C	B	R	Y	Q	K	O	L	L	U	F	A
Y	V	I	D	R	J	F	Y	A	U	B	R	N
W	E	N	V	A	Y	Q	D	P	A	E	W	C
R	G	K	P	G	R	Z	B	Y	P	T	P	Q

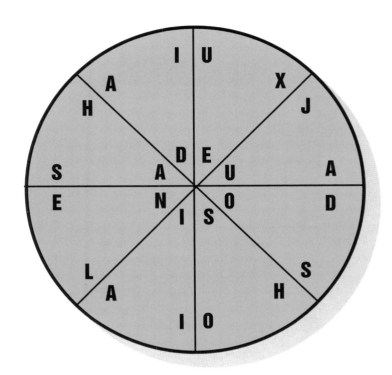

PUZZLE 157

By taking a segment and finding its pair the names of four books from the Old Testament can be made. What are they?

Answer see page 140

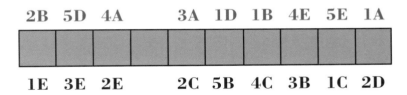

PUZZLE 158

The word frame above, when filled with the correct letters, will give the name of a pop singer. The letters are arranged in the coded square below. There are two possible alternatives to fill each square of the word frame, one correct, the other incorrect. Who is the singer?

Answer see page 140

	A	B	C	D	E
1	Y	R	V	N	B
2	P	F	M	Q	G
3	J	L	Y	W	O
4	B	U	K	C	S
5	D	A	T	H	E

PUZZLE 159

Can you work out what letter needs to be inserted in the middle to form four famous composers by combining opposite segments?

Answer see page 140

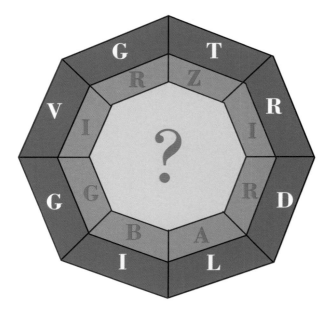

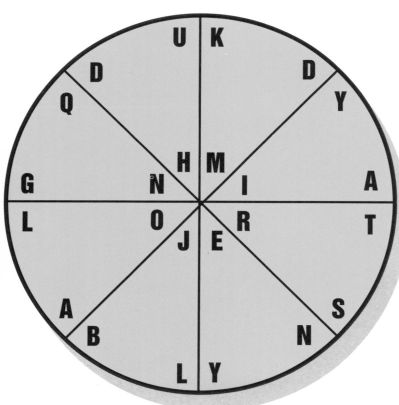

PUZZLE 160

Collect one letter from each segment to give the name of an American state. What is it?

Answer see page 140

PUZZLE 161

What letter is missing from the end turret?
Clue: Actors

Answer see page 140

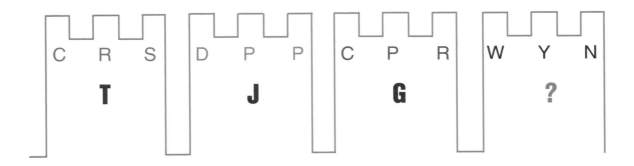

PUZZLE 162

Two sides of this pyramid can be seen, but the other two are obscured. Two eight-letter country names are written around the pyramid. What are they?

Answer see page 140

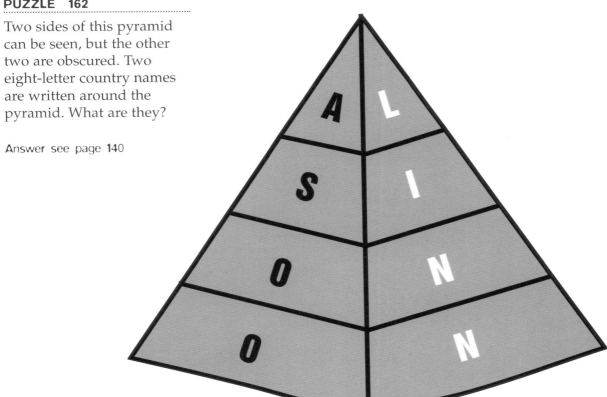

	1	2	3	4	5
A	C	I	I	N	L
B	O	L	E	N	N
C	E	E	N	S	E
D	L	T	U	S	B
E	S	T	E	W	I

PUZZLE 163

A knight, which moves either one square horizontally and two vertically or two horizontally and one vertically, is positioned on this unusual chess board at position A1. Move to each square once in the correct sequence to find the names of four famous scientists.

Answer see page 140

PUZZLE 164

This is an unusual maze. Find four separate routes through the maze without any route crossing another, although they may share the same path. On each route collect seven letters only to give you the names of four books in the Old Testament.

Answer see page 140

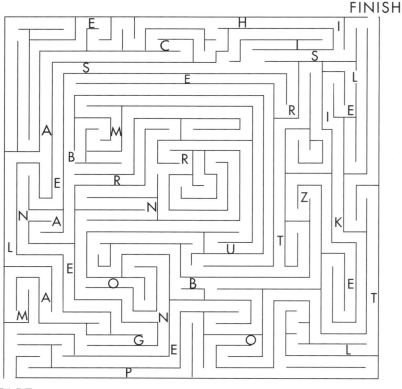

FINISH

START

PUZZLE 165

The names of the following ten champagnes can be found in this grid on vertical, horizontal and diagonal lines. Can you find them?

Answer see page 140

Ayala
Bollinger
De Venoge
Deutz
Gosset
Henriot
Lanson
Pol Roger
Ruinart
Salon

D	G	J	B	F	H	C	L	G	B
D	E	U	T	Z	E	A	A	O	M
C	T	V	H	W	N	P	L	S	F
P	R	V	E	S	R	L	A	S	H
S	A	L	O	N	I	Q	Y	E	K
K	N	N	J	N	O	X	A	T	D
B	I	W	G	V	T	G	Q	B	W
D	U	E	Z	K	F	X	E	Y	G
F	R	E	G	O	R	L	O	P	Y
Q	G	X	V	C	H	X	Z	O	D

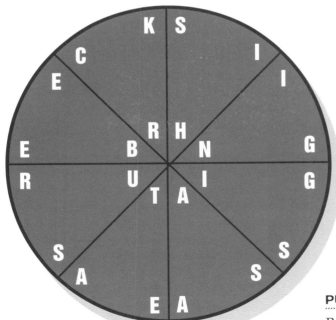

PUZZLE 166

By taking a segment and finding its pair the names of four tennis stars can be found. Who are they?

Answer see page 140

PUZZLE 167

Answer see page 140

If the name WOODROW WILSON is

Who are the other U.S. Presidents?

1.

2.

3.

4.

5.

6.

PUZZLE 168

The word frame, when filled with the correct letters, will give the name of a tennis player. The letters are arranged in the coded square below. There are two possible alternatives to fill each square of the word frame, one correct, the other incorrect. Who is the tennis player?

Answer see page 140

	A	B	C	D	E
1	N	W	I	O	M
2	R	C	G	D	A
3	H	F	Y	L	V
4	S	A	L	C	E
5	T	K	E	P	H

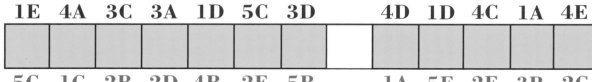

1E	4A	3C	3A	1D	5C	3D		4D	1D	4C	1A	4E
5C	1C	2B	2D	4B	2E	5B		1A	5E	2E	3B	2C

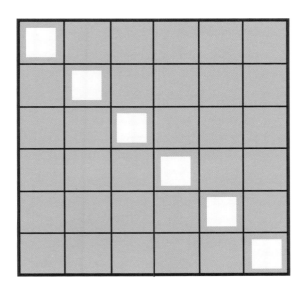

PUZZLE 169

Rearrange the order of these six famous actors' second names to give the name of another famous actor in the shaded diagonal line.

Steve MARTIN, Andy GARCIA,

Gary COOPER, Eddie MURPHY,

Keanu REEVES, Lee MARVIN.

Who is the actor given in the diagonal?

Answer see page 140

PUZZLE 170

Can you work out what letter needs to be inserted in the middle to form four capital cities by combining opposite segments?

Answer see page 141

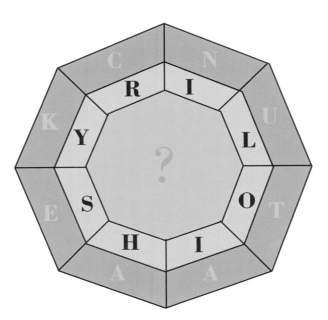

PUZZLE 171

Which well-known
expression is represented
by this rebus?

Answer see page **141**

P<u>IN</u>K

PUZZLE 172

Which well-known expression is
represented by this rebus?

Answer see page **141**

C

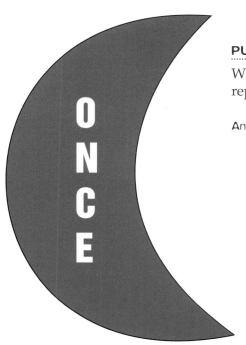

PUZZLE 173

Which well-known expression is represented by this rebus?

Answer see page 141

PUZZLE 174

Which of these groups of colors is the odd one out?

Answer see page 141

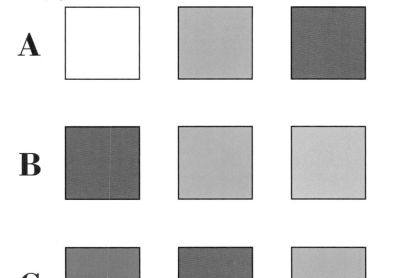

PUZZLE 175

Take one letter from each segment to find the name of a Canadian city. What is it?

Answer see page 141

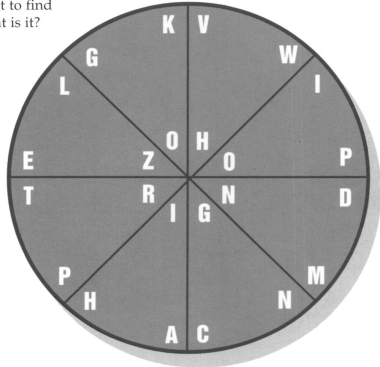

PUZZLE 176

What letters are missing from the end boxes?

Answer see page 141

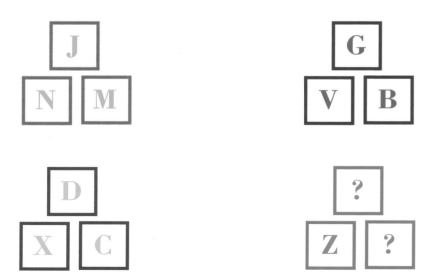

I	R	P	I	O
B	C	G	E	A
E	L		Y	B
I	A	T	L	D
U	L	N	M	O

PUZZLE 177

A knight, which moves either one square horizontally and two vertically or two horizontally and one vertically, starts at the shaded square of this small chess board visiting each square without returning to the same square twice. Find the route which spells out four famous cartoon characters.

Answer see page 141

PUZZLE 178

The maze on the right contains four names of actors and actresses. Find four separate routes through the maze without any route crossing another, although they may merge. On each route collect six letters only to give you the names of the four actors and actresses.

Answer see page 141

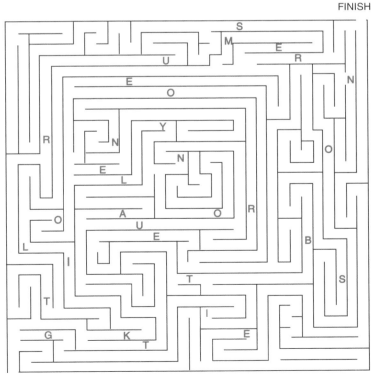

FINISH

START

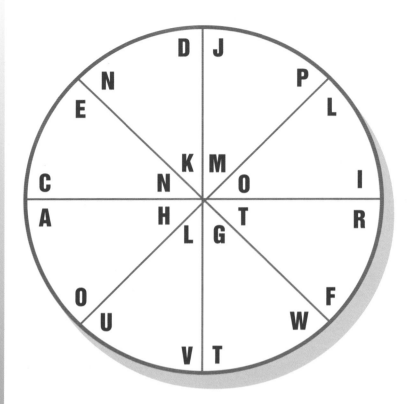

PUZZLE 179

Take one letter from each segment to find the name of a city in the USA. What is it?

Answer see page 141

PUZZLE 180

The letters surrounding each triangle are the consonants of a famous sports person's name. The letters inside the triangle have a connection with each person. What letter should replace the question mark in the fourth triangle?

Answer see page 141

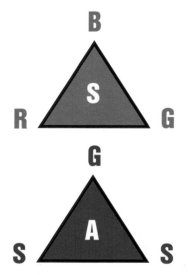

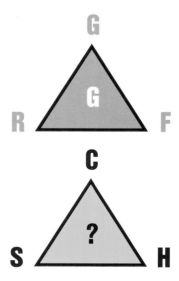

PUZZLE 181

A knight, which moves either one square horizontally and two vertically or two horizontally and one vertically, starts at the shaded square of this small chessboard visiting each square without returning to the same square twice. Find the route which spells out six names of books in the Old Testament.

Answer see page 141

L	N	H	A	R	D
U	I	E	A	S	S
I	E	O	A	H	E
J	A	E	A	I	D
S	S	X	U	H	M
E	L	T	U	O	S

FINISH

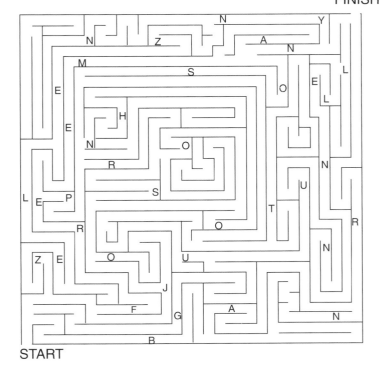

START

PUZZLE 182

This is an unusual maze. Find four separate routes through it without any route crossing another, although they may merge. On each route collect seven letters only to give you four athletes.

Answer see page 142

PUZZLE 183

Answer see page 142

If the word Presidents is

Who are the other Presidents?

PUZZLE 184

The names of the following ten fashion designers can be found in this grid on vertical, horizontal and diagonal lines. Can you find them?

Answer see page 142

Giorgio Armani
Calvin Klein
Hugo Boss
Bruce Oldfield
Jasper Conran
Red or Dead
Ellesse
Stussy
Gucci
Gianni Versace

Y	N	J	Z	B	W	K	X	B	T	N	F	G
G	I	O	R	G	I	O	A	R	M	A	N	I
T	E	S	S	O	B	O	G	U	H	R	G	A
X	L	V	E	S	V	R	Y	C	R	N	B	N
R	K	Q	S	H	F	X	B	E	V	O	K	N
Z	N	G	S	W	L	J	D	O	Q	C	M	I
J	I	T	E	M	P	O	F	L	W	R	Q	V
Y	V	K	L	R	S	B	D	Z	E	S	E	
W	L	N	L	D	B	H	P	F	Q	P	D	R
F	A	T	E	G	U	C	C	I	X	S	Y	S
X	C	A	L	T	P	Q	M	E	H	A	W	A
V	D	G	J	V	Z	D	Y	L	G	J	Z	C
S	T	U	S	S	Y	F	K	D	B	J	B	E

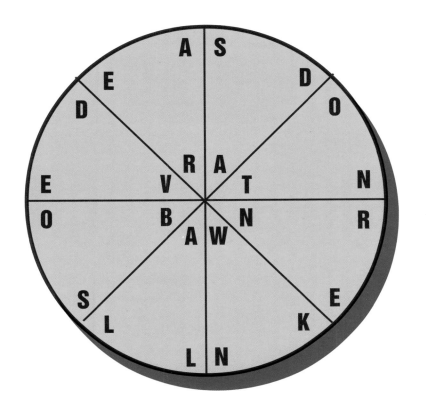

PUZZLE 185

By taking a segment and finding its pair the names of four cities of the USA can be made. What are they?

Answer see page 142

PUZZLE 186

The names of three musical terms have been merged together here. What are they?

Answer see page 142

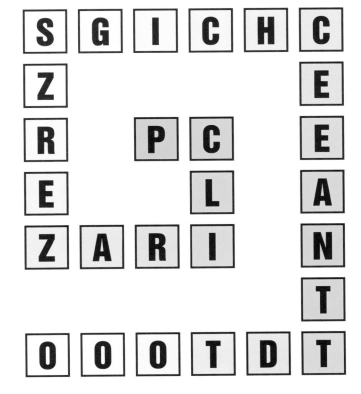

PUZZLE 187

Answer see page 142

If the country United States is

♈ ♌ ☿ ♓ ♄ ♈   ♑ ♓ ☉ ♓ ♄ ♑

Which are these states?

1. ♋ ☿ ♌ ♌ ♄ ♑ ♍ ♓ ☉

2. ♓ ♄ ✕ ☉ ♑

3. ☉ ♊ ☉ ♑ ☿ ☉

4. ♄ ☉ ♊ ☿ ☿ ♍ ↗ ♌ ☿ ☉

5. ☿ ♊ ♍ ↗ ☿ ♈ ☉

6. ♊ ♍ ♈ ☿ ♑ ☿ ☉ ♌ ☉

PUZZLE 188

The word frame below, when filled with the correct letters, will give the name of an athlete. The letters are arranged in the coded square below. There are two possible alternatives to fill each square of the word frame, one correct, the other incorrect. Who is the athlete?

Answer see page 142

	1B	1A	1D	5C
	2A	4A	2A	3B

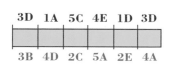

	3D	1A	5C	4E	1D	3D
	3B	4D	2C	5A	2E	4A

	A	B	C	D	E
1	E	B	U	I	F
2	G	Q	V	J	R
3	H	D	T	S	C
4	A	T	K	U	E
5	L	N	L	P	U

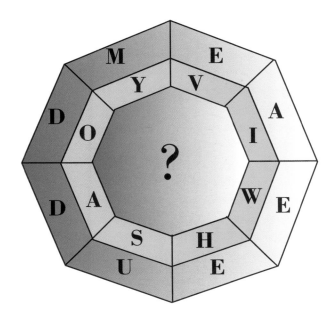

PUZZLE 189

Can you work out what letter needs to be inserted in the middle to form four ancient gods, by combining opposite segments?

Answer see page 142

PUZZLE 190

Complete the square using the letters in B R Y A N in each row. When completed no row, column or diagonal line will contain the same letter more than once. One horizontal line will spell the name correctly. What letter should replace the question mark?

Answer see page 142

				N
	N	B		
		A	N	
			Y	
?				

PUZZLE 191

Is it possible to continue the series?

Answer see page 142

PUZZLE 192

What color completes the last segment?

Answer see page 142

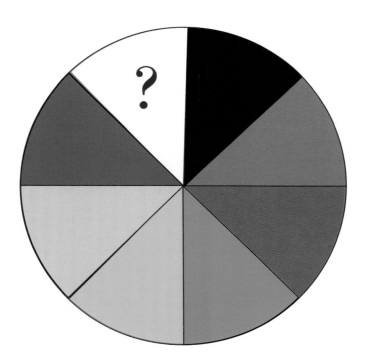

PUZZLE 193

One of these colors is wrong. Which is it
and what should it be?

Answer see page 142

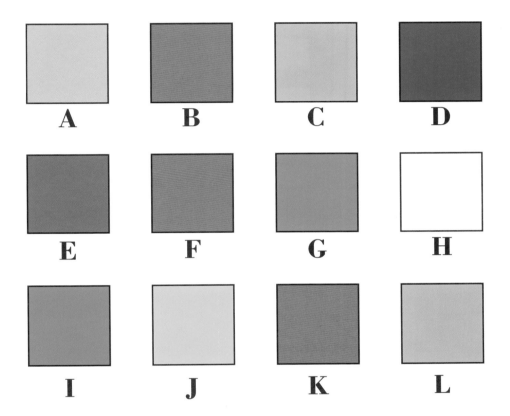

PUZZLE 194

What color completes the series?

Answer see page 142

PUZZLE 195

What is yellow worth?

Answer see page 142

PUZZLE 196

What color replaces the
question mark?

Answer see page 142

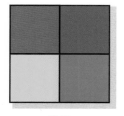

23

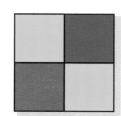

19

27

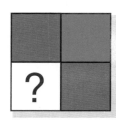

18

PUZZLE 197

Take one letter from each segment to find the name of a film star. Who is it?

Answer see page 142

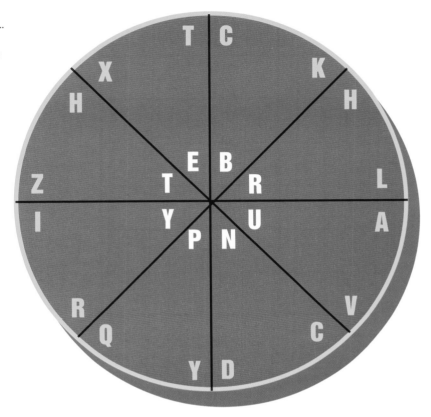

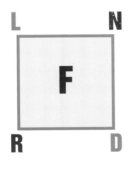

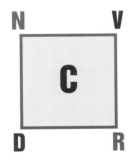

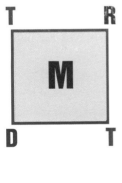

PUZZLE 198

What letter is missing from the boxes below?

Answer see page 142

A	E	W	N	S	K	L
R	N	M	N	I	E	H
H	I	A	R	P	D	I
E	A	E	S	J	A	A
L	P	E	S	A	N	E
C	T	T	I	O	U	K
E	L	S	S	E	W	G

PUZZLE 199

A knight, which moves either one square horizontally and two vertically or two horizontally and one vertically, starts at the shaded square of this small chess board visiting each square without returning to the same square twice. Find the route that spells out four famous writers.

Answer see page **143**

PUZZLE 200

This is an unusual maze. Find four separate routes through it without any route crossing another, although the paths may merge. On each route collect six letters to give you four musical terms.

Answer see page **143**

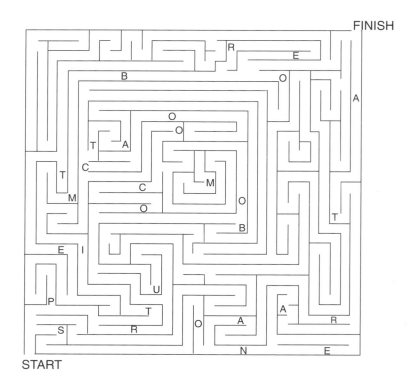

FINISH

START

PUZZLE 201

The names of the following ten furniture makers can be found in this grid on either vertical, horizontal or diagonal lines. Can you find them?

Answer see page **143**

Adam

Chippendale

Cob

Gillow

Hepplewhite

Lock

Phillipponat

Seddon

Sheraton

Stuart

T	R	Y	J	P	Q	X	G	D	H	K	X
M	A	D	N	V	R	K	F	Z	F	W	Z
J	R	N	O	D	D	E	S	Y	J	O	T
P	S	N	O	T	A	R	E	H	S	Z	F
C	H	E	P	P	L	E	W	H	I	T	E
H	C	H	I	P	P	E	N	D	A	L	E
D	M	B	Y	Z	H	I	S	C	P	G	J
F	T	A	G	W	F	T	L	Y	I	B	M
X	U	K	D	D	U	O	D	L	N	T	X
M	V	C	P	A	C	K	L	W	I	G	K
K	W	G	R	K	M	O	V	R	U	H	Y
Z	H	T	R	X	W	W	B	N	Y	K	P

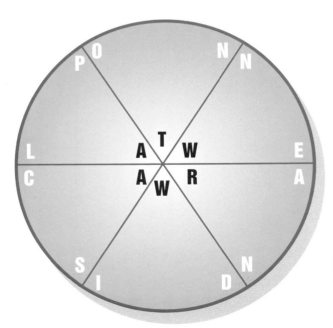

PUZZLE 202

By taking a segment and finding its pair the names of three scientists can be found. Who are they?

Answer see page **143**

PUZZLE 203

Answer see page **143**

If the names Diego Maradona and Jack Charlton are

and

Who are the other soccer players?

1.
2.
3.
4.
5.

	A	B	C	D	E
1	I	D	B	F	T
2	Y	N	Q	G	C
3	V	J	H	R	X
4	M	A	E	K	P
5	C	Z	S	O	U

PUZZLE 204

The wordframe below, when filled with the correct letters, will give the name of a US city. There are two possible letters for each square, one right and one wrong. What is the city?

Answer see page **143**

2E 3C 1A 4B 4B 2D 3A

1B 4D 2B 2E 2D 1E 5D

PUZZLE 205

What letter should appear next in this series?

Answer see page **143**

PUZZLE 206

This is an unusual maze. Find four separate routes through it without any route crossing another, although the paths may merge. On each route collect six letters to give you four scientists.
Who are they?

Answer see page **143**

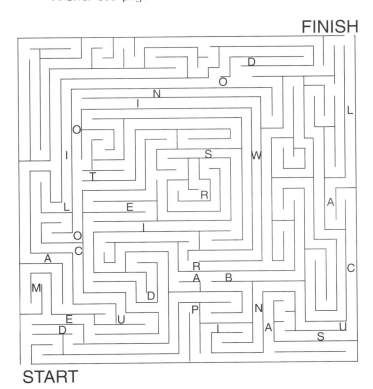

FINISH

START

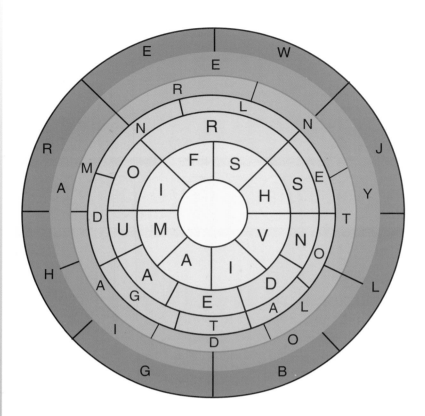

PUZZLE 207

Turn the dials on this diagram to give 8 forenames and 8 surnames of famous actresses. Then match them up to give their full names. Who are they? (A score above 5 is very good!)

Answer see page **143**

PUZZLE 208

Can you work out what letter needs to be inserted in the middle to form four airlines by combining opposite segments?

Answer see page **143**

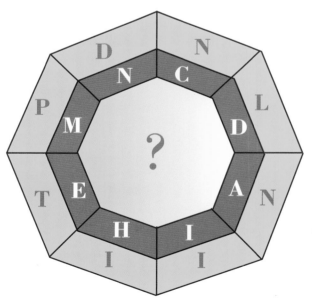

O	P	C	A	O	R	N
K	A	T	Y	I	P	D
L	M	L	R	C	N	A
R	P	I	Y	M	L	D
W	A	E	K	N	G	O
R	N	E	T	C	L	A
R	A	I	O	F	S	E

PUZZLE 209

A knight, which moves either one square horizontally and two vertically or two horizontally and one vertically, is positioned on this chess board on position B2. If you move to all the squares in the right sequence, without visiting any square twice, you will find the names of five famous golfers.

Answer see page **143**

PUZZLE 210

The names of the following ten film stars can be found in this grid on vertical, horizontal and diagonal lines. Can you find them?

Answer see page 144

John Cleese
Tom Cruise
Mel Gibson
Hugh Grant
Tom Hanks
Val Kilmer
Bruce Lee
Al Pacino
Sean Penn
Brad Pitt

W	Z	Q	E	P	R	V	H	E	F	M
T	O	U	S	Y	J	A	H	E	E	Z
T	N	S	I	G	K	L	U	L	S	W
I	I	E	U	F	H	K	G	E	E	P
P	C	A	R	H	X	I	H	C	E	H
D	A	N	C	H	B	L	G	U	L	J
A	P	P	M	S	Q	M	R	R	C	R
R	L	E	O	J	R	E	A	B	N	G
B	A	N	T	T	Z	R	N	P	H	Y
S	K	N	A	H	M	O	T	W	O	S
Y	R	B	X	F	Q	J	X	N	J	S

125

PUZZLE 211

What color should replace
the question mark?

Answer see page 144

 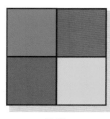 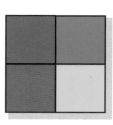 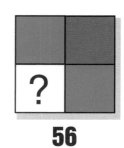

45 **49** **48** **56**

PUZZLE 212

What letter should replace
the question mark?

Answer see page 144

 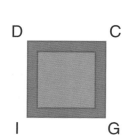 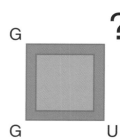

G ... Z   H ... C   D ... C   G ... ?
G ... N   N ... G   I ... G   G ... U

S  T   G  U   A  U   C  **?**

L   E   P   Y   U   R   I   T

PUZZLE 213

What letter should replace the question mark?

Answer see page **144**

A  L   B  R   F  A   E  **?**

A   E   O   M   L   E   T   H

PUZZLE 214

What letter should replace the question mark?

Answer see page **144**

PUZZLE 215

Answer see page 144

If the name Elizabeth Taylor is

Who are the other legendary film stars?

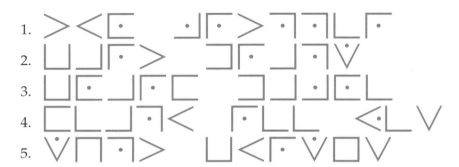

1.
2.
3.
4.
5.

PUZZLE 216

Turn the dials on this diagram to reveal 13 musical terms. A score above 8 is very good.

Answer see page 144

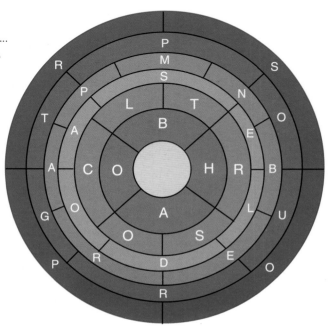

PUZZLE 217

The names of the following ten car manufacturers can be found in this grid on vertical, horizontal and diagonal lines. Can you find them?

Answer see page 144

Citroen

Jaguar

Peugeot

Renault

Rolls Royce

Rover

Skoda

Toyota

Volkswagen

Yugo

R	N	B	L	F	K	X	C	D	R
E	N	D	C	W	Q	H	S	O	E
N	E	G	A	W	S	K	L	O	V
A	O	H	J	K	O	L	B	P	O
U	R	G	V	D	S	F	Y	J	R
L	T	C	A	R	A	U	G	A	J
T	I	T	O	E	G	U	E	P	M
P	C	Y	T	O	Y	O	T	A	B
J	C	F	V	G	Z	C	W	D	K
E	K	D	P	M	H	Q	G	Y	F

PUZZLE 218

What letter has been missed from the last box?

Answer see page 144

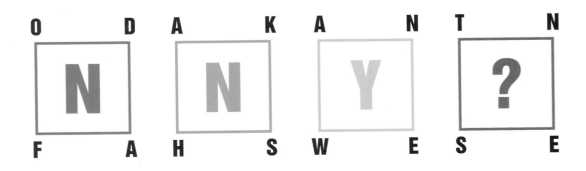

PUZZLE 219

Answer see page 144

If the term ancient gods is

Who are these gods?

1.

2.

3.

4.

5.

6.

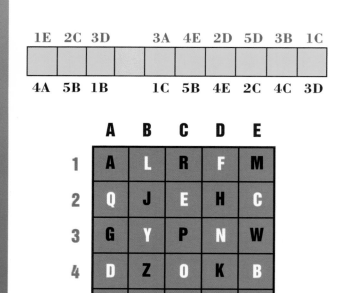

1E	2C	3D		3A	4E	2D	5D	3B	1C
4A	5B	1B		1C	5B	4E	2C	4C	3D

	A	**B**	**C**	**D**	**E**
1	A	L	R	F	M
2	Q	J	E	H	C
3	G	Y	P	N	W
4	D	Z	O	K	B
5	T	I	V	S	X

PUZZLE 220

The wordframe below, when filled with the correct letters, will give the name of a film star. The letters are arranged in the coded square below. There are two possible alternatives to fill each square of the wordframe, one correct, the other incorrect. Who is the film star?

Answer see page 144

PUZZLE 221

A knight, which moves either one square horizontally and two vertically or two horizontally and one vertically, starts at the shaded square of this chess board visiting each square without returning to the same square twice. Find the route which spells out six famous movie stars.

Answer see page 144

O	T	E	S	I	O	T	I
M	O	P	S	L	B	G	R
E	O	G	N	D	N	G	O
N	E	B	O	R	A	I	O
H	V	E	J	D	L	M	T
S	R	A	E	F	D	R	N
E	W	B	U	A	I	R	C
O	I	M	N	E	R	E	T

PUZZLE 222

The names of the following ten perfumes can be found in this grid on vertical, horizontal and diagonal lines. Can you find them?

Answer see page 144

Amarige

Anais Anais

Coco

Dune

Miss Dior

Obsession

Paris

Safari

Samsara

Spellbound

S	I	A	N	A	S	I	A	N	A
A	P	D	G	H	F	P	J	C	R
F	C	E	G	I	R	A	M	A	A
A	F	H	L	D	J	R	K	F	S
R	Y	Q	U	L	Z	I	Z	R	M
I	R	N	Z	X	B	S	F	X	A
Q	E	V	K	W	O	O	Y	J	S
B	H	K	V	D	W	C	U	G	I
O	B	S	E	S	S	I	O	N	G
R	O	I	D	S	S	I	M	C	D

131

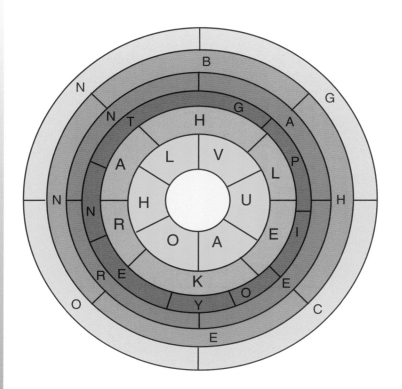

PUZZLE 223

Turn the dial on this diagram to give 11 names of lakes from around the world. (7 or over is a good score.)

Answer see page 144

PUZZLE 224

Can you work out what letter needs to be inserted in the middle to form four artists by combining opposite segments?

Answer see page 144

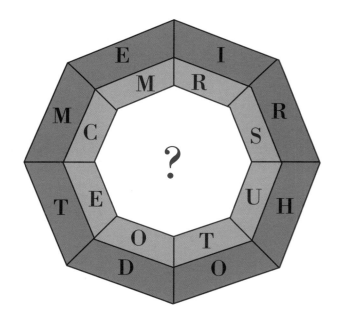

PUZZLE 225

The names of the following ten tennis players can be found in this grid on vertical, horizontal and diagonal lines. Can you find them?

Answer see page 145

C	J	H	J	K	I	M	F	G	I	M	C	W
B	E	C	M	Z	K	Y	X	B	V	N	A	Y
J	R	I	A	O	S	J	V	H	A	Y	V	S
F	E	T	R	N	D	C	Y	V	N	D	O	E
K	M	S	C	H	E	P	H	E	L	K	K	L
G	Y	L	R	D	S	K	F	P	E	J	U	E
Z	B	E	O	X	U	E	G	A	N	M	S	S
C	A	A	S	W	R	W	B	T	D	D	A	A
P	T	H	S	R	G	M	W	C	L	Z	N	C
J	E	C	E	F	E	Y	V	A	Y	B	E	I
F	S	I	T	Y	R	Z	M	S	J	X	L	N
H	R	M	P	H	G	C	B	H	K	F	E	O
A	N	T	O	V	O	N	A	N	A	J	H	M

Jeremy Bates
Pat Cash
Wayne Ferreira
Ivan Lendl
Jana Novotna
Marc Rosset
Greg Rusedski
Monica Seles
Michael Stich
Helena Sukova

PUZZLE 226

Answer see page 145

If the word scientist is

who are these scientists?

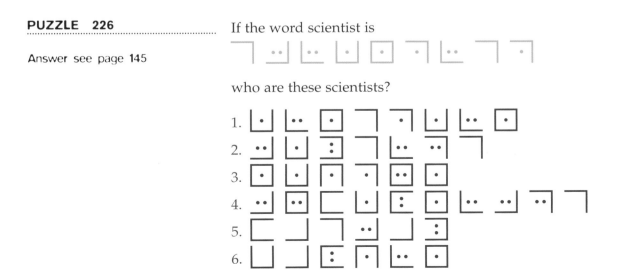

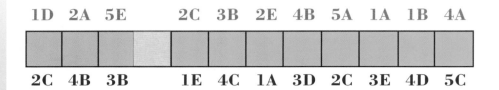

1D	2A	5E		2C	3B	2E	4B	5A	1A	1B	4A
2C	4B	3B		1E	4C	1A	3D	2C	3E	4D	5C

	A	**B**	**C**	**D**	**E**
1	G	A	B	L	S
2	I	Q	M	F	C
3	D	Z	X	O	K
4	H	J	C	W	M
5	L	V	N	P	R

PUZZLE 227

The wordframe above, when filled with the correct letters, will give the name of a female athlete. The letters are arranged in the coded square below. There are two possible alternatives to fill each square of the wordframe, one correct, the other incorrect. Who is the athlete?

Answer see page 145

PUZZLE 228

Turn the dials on this unusual safe to give 12 surnames of sports stars from the past and present. (More than 8 is a good score.)

Answer see page 145

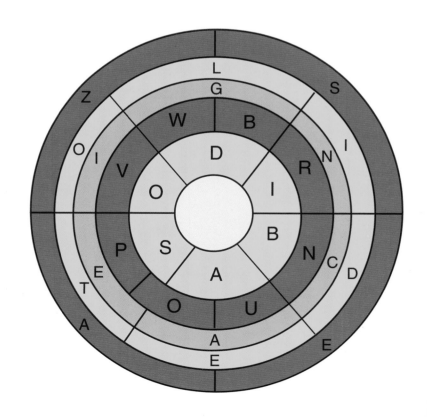

PUZZLE 229

Rearrange these boxes in a 3 x 3 square in such a way that the adjoining letters are always the same. Then add the alphanumeric values of each line of three outer letters and convert back to letters to give the name of a Roman god.

Answer see page 145

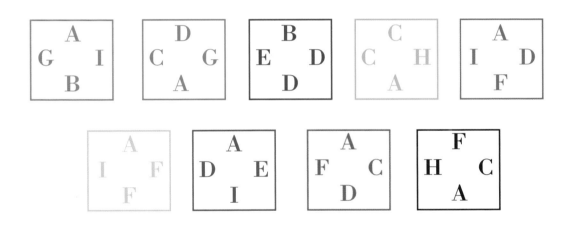

PUZZLE 230

What letters should replace the question marks?

Answer see page 145

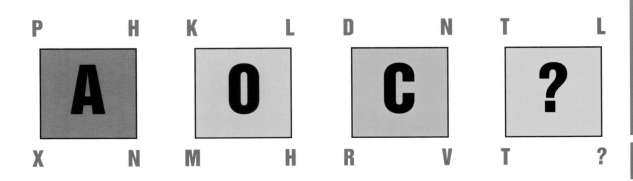

PUZZLE 231

What number replaces the question mark?

Answer see page 145

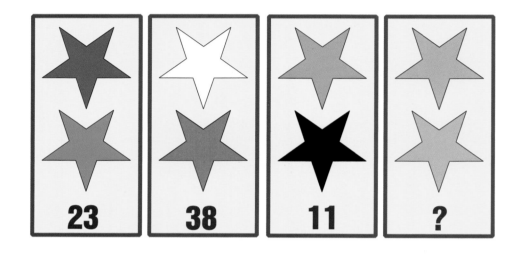

PUZZLE 232

What number replaces the question mark?

Answer see page 145

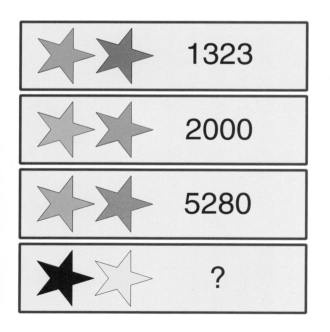

PUZZLE 233

Can one of these squares complete the sequence?

Answer see page 145

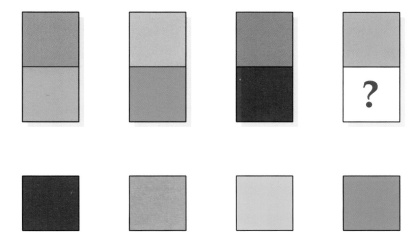

PUZZLE 234

Which square completes the sequence?

Answer see page 145

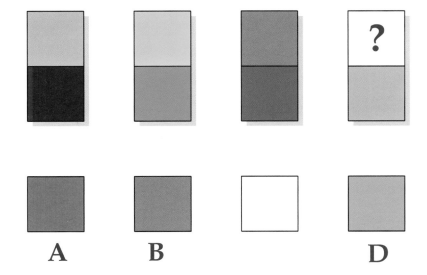

A   B   D

PUZZLE 235

Here is a strange signpost to the burial grounds in Ancient Egypt. How far is it to burial ground of Thoth?

Answer see page 145

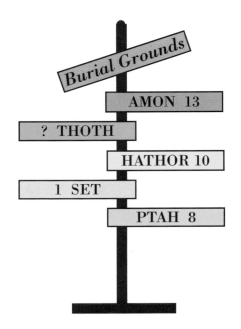

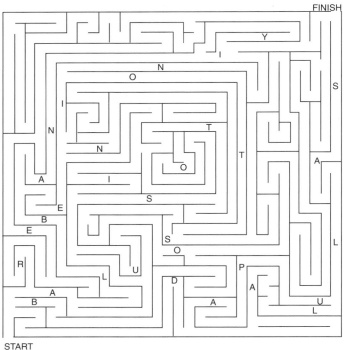

FINISH

START

PUZZLE 236

This is an unusual maze. Find four separate routes which do not cross each other, although the paths may merge. On each route collect six letters to give you four US cities.

Answer see page 145

Medium Answers

Answer 155
A. Tango, Polka, Rumba, Samba

Answer 156

T	N	A	R	G	D	N	U	M	A	S	O	R
B	Y	N	L	K	L	Q	O	X	C	B	O	A
Q	W	T	F	Z	P	H	K	U	J	R	G	Y
Y	G	H	V	S	N	X	E	O	R	R	C	M
D	V	O	W	E	M	D	I	R	S	U	K	O
J	K	N	K	D	B	P	T	T	U	N	O	N
P	M	Y	S	O	S	C	H	R	C	O	P	D
P	F	T	Y	H	A	Y	F	E	O	L	J	B
Z	W	O	U	R	Z	G	L	B	B	O	C	L
F	C	B	R	Y	Q	K	O	L	L	U	F	A
Y	V	E	D	R	J	F	Y	A	U	B	R	N
W	E	N	V	A	Y	Q	D	P	A	E	W	C
R	G	K	P	G	R	Z	B	Y	P	T	P	Q

Answer 157
Daniel, Exodus, Isaiah and Joshua can be found by pairing alternate segments.

Answer 158
Bob Marley.

Answer 159
E. Elgar, Bizet, Grieg, Verdi

Answer 160
Maryland.

Answer 161
J. The vowels have been omitted from the surnames and the initial of the first name is in the middle of the box: Tom Cruise, Johnny Depp, Gary Cooper and John Wayne.

Answer 162
Malaysia and Hong Kong.

Answer 163
The scientists are: Celsius, Einstein, Bell, Newton.

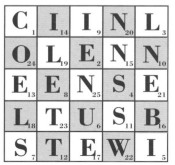

Answer 164
Malachi, Genesis, Numbers, Ezekiel
The last letter of two of the four names is the same.

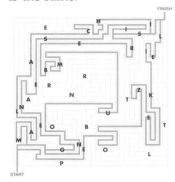

Answer 165

D	G	J	B	F	H	C	L	G	B
D	E	U	T	Z	E	A	A	O	M
C	T	Y	H	W	N	P	L	S	F
P	R	V	E	S	R	L	A	S	H
S	A	L	O	N	I	Q	Y	E	K
K	N	N	J	N	O	X	A	T	D
B	I	W	G	V	T	G	Q	B	W
D	U	E	Z	K	F	X	E	Y	G
F	R	E	G	O	R	L	O	P	Y
Q	G	X	V	C	H	X	Z	O	D

Answer 166
Agassi, Becker, Hingis, Muster.

Answer 167
1. Bill Clinton 2. Abraham Lincoln
3. George Washington 4. Harry S. Truman
5. John F. Kennedy 6. Ulysses Grant

Answer 168
Michael Chang.

Answer 169
Tony Curtis.

C	O	O	P	E	R
M	U	R	P	H	Y
M	A	R	V	I	N
M	A	R	T	I	N
G	A	R	C	I	A
R	E	E	V	E	S

Answer 170
O. Cairo, Hanoi, Seoul, Tokyo

Answer 171
In the pink.

Answer 172
Deep blue sea.

Answer 173
Once in a blue moon.

Answer 174
A. The initial letters of the others make words (ROPY,GROW).

Answer 175
Winnipeg.

Answer 176

Answer 177
The cartoon characters are: Bambi, Cinderella, Pluto and Yogi.

I 24	R 11	P 16	I 5	O 22
B 1	C 6	G 23	E 10	A 15
E 12	L 17		Y 21	B 4
I 7	A 2	T 19	L 14	D 9
U 18	L 13	N 8	M 3	O 20

Answer 178
Turner, Kilmer, Taylor, Gibson
The first letter of two of the routes is the same, and the last letter of three of the routes is the same.

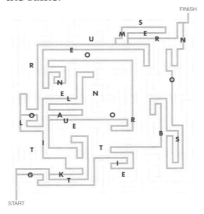

Answer 179
Portland.

Answer 180
A. The letters outside are consonants of famous tennis players. They are: (top)Borg and Graf, (bottom) Agassi and Cash. The letters inside the triangles are the initials of their nationality. They are Swedish, German, American and Australian respectively.

Answer 181
The books are: Samuel, Joshua, Exodus, Isaiah, Daniel and Esther.

L 30	N 27	H 10	A 23	R 36	D 25
U 11	I 22	E 29	A 26	S 9	S 20
I 28	E 31	O 8	A 21	H 24	E 35
J 7	A 12	E 5	A 2	I 19	D 16
S 32	S 1	X 14	U 17	H 34	M 3
E 13	L 6	T 33	U 4	O 15	S 18

Answer 182
Gunnell, Freeman, Johnson, Zelezny
The last letter of two of the routes is the same.

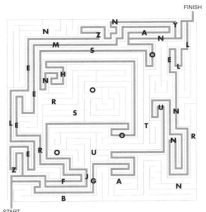

Answer 183
1. Carter 2. Eisenhower 3. Johnson,
4. Reagan 5. Roosevelt

Answer 184

Y	N	J	Z	B	W	K	X	B	T	N	F	G
G	I	O	R	G	I	O	A	R	M	A	N	I
T	E	S	S	O	B	O	G	U	H	R	G	A
X	L	V	E	S	V	R	Y	C	R	N	B	N
R	K	Q	S	H	F	X	B	E	V	O	K	N
Z	N	G	S	W	L	J	D	O	Q	C	M	I
J	I	T	E	M	P	O	F	L	W	R	Q	I
Y	V	K	L	K	R	S	B	D	Z	E	S	E
W	L	N	L	D	B	H	P	F	Q	P	D	R
F	A	T	E	G	U	C	C	I	X	S	Y	S
X	C	A	L	T	P	Q	M	E	H	A	W	A
V	D	G	J	V	Z	D	Y	L	G	J	Z	C
S	T	U	S	S	Y	F	K	D	B	J	B	E

Answer 185
Boston, Dallas, Denver and Newark can be found by pairing opposite segments.

Answer 186
Pizzicato, Crescendo, Larghetto

Answer 187
1. Minnesota 2. Texas 3. Alaska
4. California 5. Florida 6. Louisiana

Answer 188
Gail Devers.

Answer 189
N. Hymen, Venus, Diana, Woden

Answer 190
Y.

B	R	Y	A	N
A	N	B	R	Y
R	Y	A	N	B
N	B	R	Y	A
Y	A	N	B	R

Answer 191
Yes, a seven-letter color such as scarlet or magenta would do it.

Answer 192
Red. The colors are in alphabetical order going clockwise.

Answer 193
G should be orange (then the initials in each line would make a word - PROP, BROW, GYRO).

Answer 194
Red. The colors are in a repeating alphabetical order.

Answer 195
7

Answer 196
Yellow (the numbers are added to give the totals).

Answer 197
Brad Pitt.

Answer 198
T. The cities, without vowels and the initial of the states they are in. Orlando (Florida), Detroit (Michigan), Denver (Colorado) and Dallas (Texas).

142

Answer 199

The great writers are: Stephen King, Oscar Wilde, William Shakespeare and Jane Austen.

A$_{27}$	E$_{6}$	W$_{17}$	N$_{42}$	S$_{29}$	K$_{8}$	L$_{19}$
R$_{16}$	N$_{49}$	M$_{28}$	N$_{7}$	I$_{18}$	E$_{43}$	H$_{30}$
H$_{5}$	I$_{26}$	A$_{41}$	R$_{38}$	P$_{35}$	D$_{20}$	I$_{9}$
E$_{48}$	A$_{15}$	E$_{36}$	S$_{1}$	J$_{40}$	A$_{31}$	A$_{44}$
L$_{25}$	P$_{4}$	E$_{39}$	S$_{34}$	A$_{37}$	N$_{10}$	E$_{21}$
C$_{14}$	T$_{47}$	T$_{2}$	I$_{23}$	O$_{12}$	U$_{45}$	K$_{32}$
E$_{3}$	L$_{24}$	S$_{13}$	S$_{46}$	E$_{33}$	W$_{22}$	G$_{11}$

Answer 200

Rococo, Rubato, Sonata, Timbre
The first letter of two of the routes is the same and the last letter of two of the routes is the same.

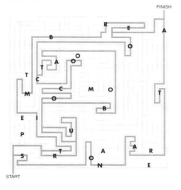

Answer 201

T	R	Y	J	P	Q	X	G	D	H	K	X
M	A	D	N	V	R	K	F	Z	F	W	Z
J	R	N	O	D	D	E	S	Y	J	O	T
P	S	N	O	T	A	R	E	H	S	Z	F
C	H	E	P	P	L	E	W	H	I	T	E
H	C	H	I	P	P	E	N	D	A	L	E
D	M	B	Y	Z	H	I	S	C	P	G	J
F	T	A	G	W	F	T	L	Y	I	B	M
X	U	K	D	D	U	O	D	L	N	T	X
M	V	C	P	A	C	K	L	W	I	G	K
K	W	G	R	K	M	O	V	R	U	H	Y
Z	H	T	R	X	W	W	B	N	Y	K	P

Answer 202

Darwin, Newton and Pascal can be found by pairing adjacent segments.

Answer 203

1) Roberto Baggio 2) Dennis Bergkamp
3) Kevin Keegan 4) Eric Cantona
5) Jurgen Klinsmann

Answer 204

Chicago.

Answer 205

Z. Each letter is one alphabetical place after the number.

Answer 206

Edison, Darwin, Euclid, Pascal
The first letter of two of the routes is the same and the last letter of two of the routes is the same.

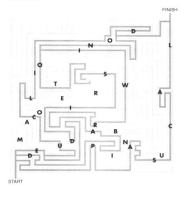

Answer 207

Holly Hunter, Sally Field, Daryl Hannah, Meg Ryan, Demi Moore, Winona Ryder, Jane Fonda, Bette Davis.

Answer 208

A. India, China, Delta, Pan Am

Answer 209

The golfers are: Arnold Palmer, Nick Faldo, Tom Watson, Nick Price and Gary Player.

O$_{23}$	P$_{44}$	C$_{33}$	A$_{8}$	O$_{21}$	R$_{42}$	N$_{31}$
K$_{34}$	A$_{1}$	T$_{22}$	Y$_{43}$	I$_{32}$	P$_{7}$	D$_{20}$
L$_{45}$	M$_{24}$	L$_{9}$	R$_{12}$	C$_{15}$	N$_{30}$	A$_{41}$
R$_{2}$	P$_{35}$	I$_{14}$	Y$_{47}$	M$_{10}$	L$_{19}$	D$_{6}$
W$_{25}$	A$_{46}$	E$_{48}$	K$_{16}$	N$_{13}$	G$_{40}$	O$_{29}$
R$_{36}$	N$_{3}$	E$_{48}$	T$_{27}$	C$_{38}$	L$_{5}$	A$_{18}$
R$_{49}$	A$_{26}$	I$_{37}$	O$_{4}$	F$_{17}$	S$_{28}$	E$_{39}$

Answer 210

W	Z	Q	E	P	R	V	H	E	F	M
T	O	U	S	Y	J	A	H	E	E	Z
T	N	S	I	G	K	L	U	L	S	W
I	I	E	U	F	H	K	G	E	E	P
P	C	A	R	H	X	I	H	C	E	H
D	A	N	C	H	B	L	G	U	L	J
A	P	P	M	S	Q	M	R	R	C	R
R	L	E	O	J	R	E	A	B	N	G
B	A	N	T	T	Z	R	N	P	H	Y
S	K	N	A	H	M	O	T	W	O	S
Y	R	B	X	F	Q	J	X	N	J	S

Answer 211

Blue (add the top numbers, then the bottom ones, and multiply).

Answer 212

F. The letters at the corners are moved two places in the alphabet. Then you get the words EXPEL, FABLE, BARGE, EDGES.

Answer 213

U. This gives the words STYLE, GUPPY, AUGUR, CUBIT.

Answer 214

A. (this gives ALGAE, BROOM, FABLE, EARTH).

Answer 215

1. Yul Brynner 2. Cary Grant 3. Clark Gable 4. Keanu Reaves 5. Tony Curtis

Answer 216

Alto, Bass, Chord, Largo, Lento, Opera, Opus, Presto, Rondo, Rubato, Sonato, Tempo, Tenor.

Answer 217

R	N	B	L	F	K	X	C	D	R
E	N	D	C	W	Q	H	S	O	E
N	E	G	A	W	S	K	L	O	V
A	O	H	J	K	O	L	B	P	O
U	R	G	V	D	S	F	Y	J	R
L	T	C	A	R	A	U	G	A	J
T	I	T	O	E	G	U	E	P	M
P	C	Y	T	O	Y	O	T	A	B
J	C	F	V	G	Z	C	W	D	K
E	K	D	P	M	H	Q	G	Y	F

Answer 218

O. The middle letter of each name is in the middle of the box. Fonda, Hanks, Wayne and Stone.

Answer 219

1. Odin 2. Hermes 3. Osiris 4. Poseidon 5. Athena 6. Cupid.

Answer 220

Mel Gibson.

Answer 221

The stars are: Tom Cruise, Mel Gibson, Robert De Niro, Steve Martin, Whoopi Goldberg, and Jane Fonda.

O 45	T 32	E 11	S 16	I 47	O 30	T 1	I 14
M 10	O 17	P 46	S 31	L 12	B 15	G 48	R 29
E 33	O 44	G 55	N 58	D 51	N 62	G 13	O 2
N 18	E 9	B 52	O 61	R 54	A 57	I 28	O 49
H 43	V 34	E 59	J 56	D 63	L 50	M	T 24
S 8	R 19	A 64	E 53	F 60	D 25	R 38	N 27
E 35	W 42	B 21	U 6	A 37	I 40	R 23	C 4
O 20	I 7	M 36	N 41	E 22	R 5	E 26	T 39

Answer 222

S	I	A	N	A	S	I	A	N	A
A	P	D	G	H	F	P	J	C	R
F	C	E	G	I	R	A	M	A	A
A	F	H	L	D	J	R	K	F	S
R	Y	Q	U	L	Z	I	Z	R	M
I	R	N	Z	X	B	S	F	X	A
Q	E	V	K	W	O	O	Y	J	S
B	H	K	V	D	W	C	U	G	I
O	B	S	E	S	S	I	O	N	G
R	O	I	D	S	S	I	M	C	D

Answer 223

Huron, Erie, Apal, Baykal, Cha, Onega, Eyre, Erne, Neagh, Volta, Geneva.

Answer 224

N. Monet, Rodin, Munch, Ernst

Answer 225

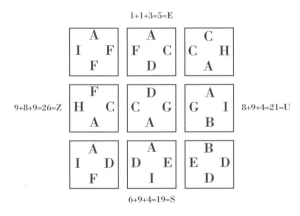

Answer 226
1. Einstein 2. Celsius 3. Newton
4. Copernicus 5. Pascal 6. Darwin

Answer 227
Liz McColgan.

Answer 228
Spitz, Borg, Bowe, Lewis, Ali, Pele, Zico, Senna, Lauda, Bats, David, Coe.

Answer 229
Zeus.

1+1+3=5=E

9+8+9=26=Z

8+9+4=21=U

6+9+4=19=S

A I F	A F C D	C C H A
F H C A	D C G A	A G I B
A I F	A D E I	B E E D D

Answer 230

G
N

The letters read clockwise from the top left are the consonants in the state capitals and the state's initial is in the middle. Phoenix in Arizona, Oklahoma (City) in Oklahoma, Denver in Colorado and Atlanta in Georgia.

Answer 231
10. (The colors are turned into a number by taking the alphanumeric values of the letters. Then subtract.)

Answer 232
2668 (alphanumeric values multiplied).

Answer 233
No. Totals for the pairs (using the number of letters in each color) are 7, 9, 11. It is not possible to make 13.

Answer 234
C. Pairs add up to 11 letters.

Answer 235
12. The number of letters between the alphanumeric position of the first and last letters of each name.

Answer 236
Albany, Austin, Dallas, Boston
The first letter of two of the routes is the same and the last letter of two of the routes is the same.

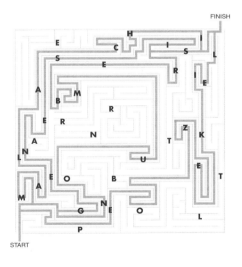

Hard

Puzzles

PUZZLE 237

Draw three straight lines that will give you six sections with 1 clock, 2 hares and 3 lightning bolts in each section. The lines do not have to go from one edge to another.

Answer see page 242

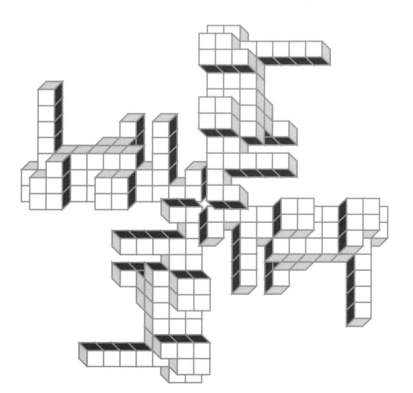

PUZZLE 238

This figure is a collection of blocks rotated through four perspectives. How many blocks are there in total? There are no gaps between the invisible blocks

Answer see page 242

148

PUZZLE 239

Which two of these butterflies are identical?

Answer see page 242

A   B

C   D

E   F

PUZZLE 240

Which of the following is the odd one out?

Answer see page 242

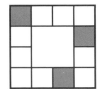 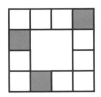 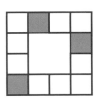 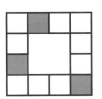

PUZZLE 241

Which panel fills the gap?

Answer see page 242

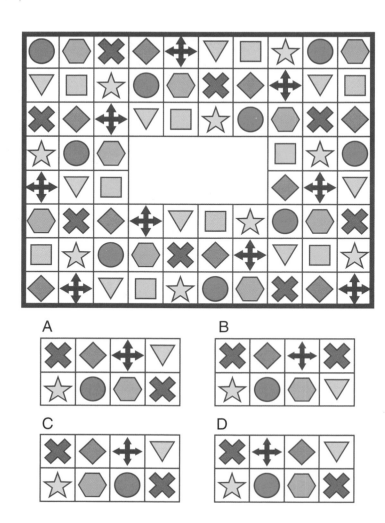

PUZZLE 242

Which of the following is the odd one out?

Answer see page 242

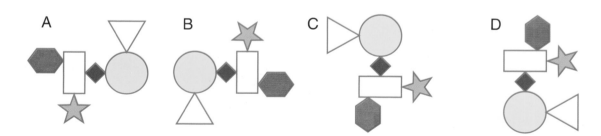

PUZZLE 243

Which of the following penguins is the odd one out?

Answer see page 242

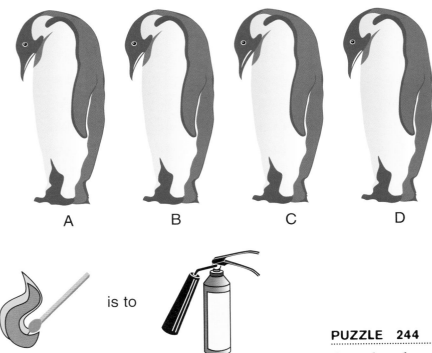

A   B   C   D

PUZZLE 244

Complete the analogy.

Answer see page 242

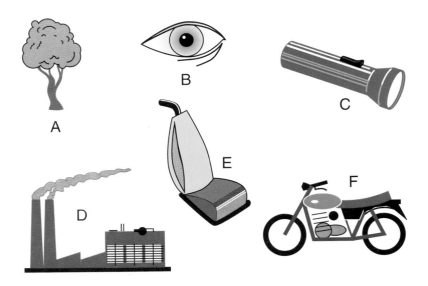

is to

as DIRT is to

A

B

C

D

E

F

PUZZLE 245

Which of the following is
the odd one out?

Answer see page 242

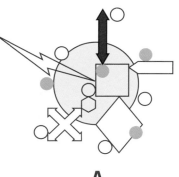

A

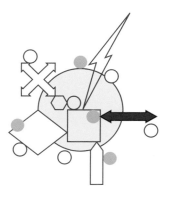

B

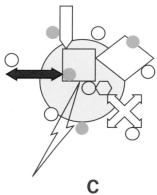

C

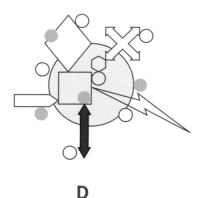

D

PUZZLE 246

How many yellow spotted tiles are
missing from this design?

Answer see page 242

PUZZLE 247

If the black arrow pulls in
the direction indicated, will
the load rise or fall?

Answer see page 242

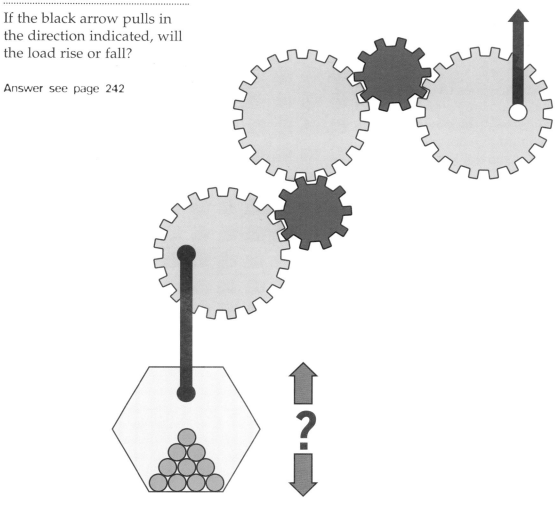

PUZZLE 248

Which two birds are identical?

Answer see page 242

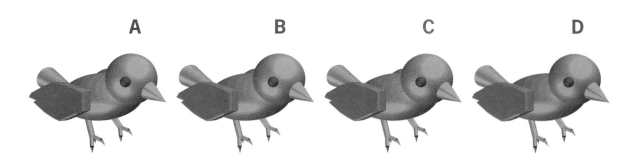

A   B   C   D

PUZZLE 249

When old gardener Lincoln died, he left his grandchildren 19 rose bushes each. The grandchildren, Agnes (A), Billy (B), Catriona (C) and Derek (D), hated each other, and so decided to fence off their plots as shown. Who had to build the greatest run of fence?

Answer see page 242

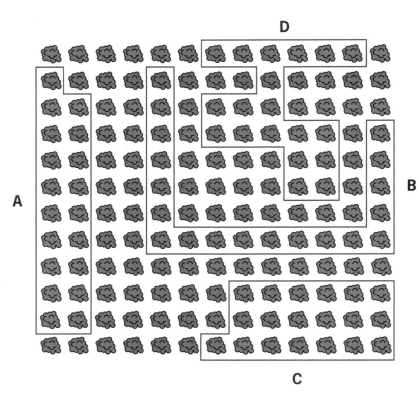

PUZZLE 250

Which of these spiders and their webs make two identical pairs?

Answer see page 242

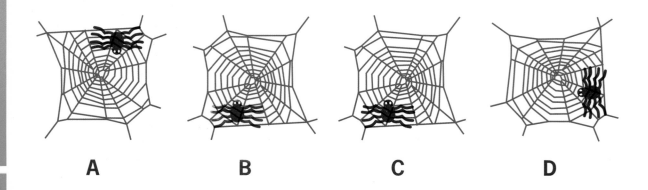

| A | B | C | D |

PUZZLE 251

Which of the following is the odd one out?

Answer see page 242

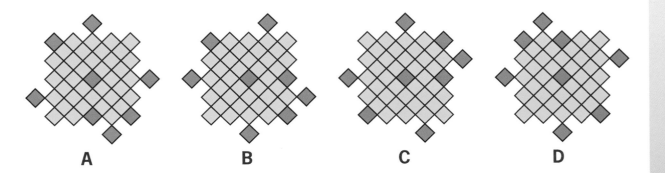

A   B   C   D

PUZZLE 252

Spot the 10 differences in picture B.

Answer see page 242

A   B

PUZZLE 253

Shade in this map of the Upper Plains –
Great Lakes States using no more than 4
tints, so that no adjacent states have the
same hue.

Answer see page 243

PUZZLE 254

Which of the following is the odd one out?

Answer see page 243

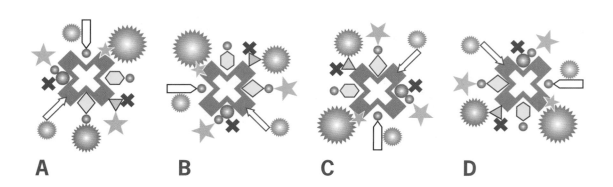

A   B   C   D

PUZZLE 255

Which of the following is the odd one out?

Answer see page 243

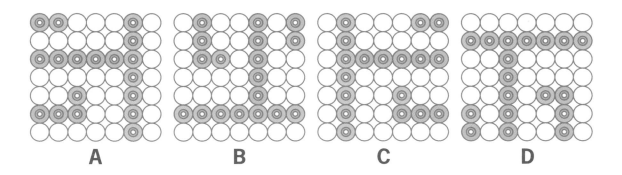

A   B   C   D

PUZZLE 256

How many bricks are missing from this wall?

Answer see page 243

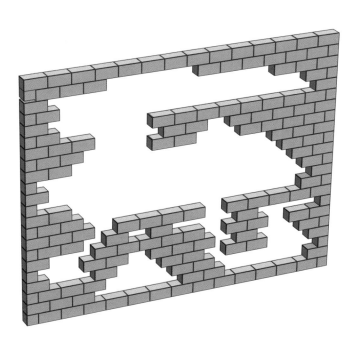

PUZZLE 257

Which of the following is the odd one out?

Answer see page 243

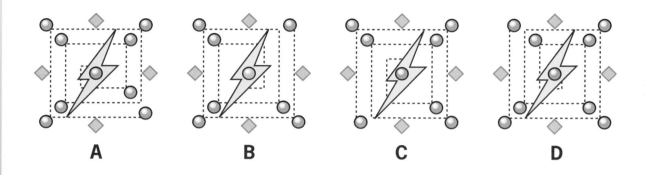

PUZZLE 258

Which shape should replace the question mark, A, B, C, or D?

Answer see page 243

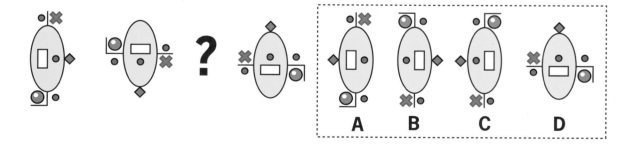

PUZZLE 259

Complete the analogy.

Answer see page 243

is to

as

is to

A

B

C

D

E

F

G

H

PUZZLE 260

Which of the following is the odd one out?

Answer see page 243

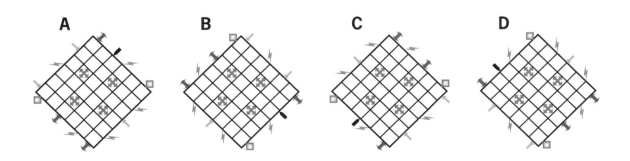

A   B   C   D

PUZZLE 261

There is something wrong
with one of the items in a
set. Which one?

Answer see page 243

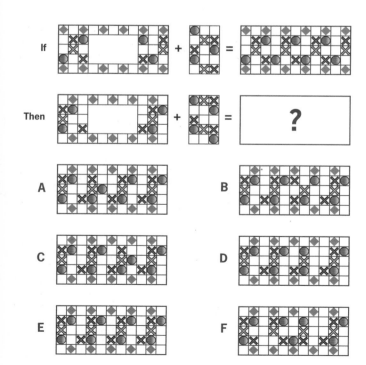

PUZZLE 262

Complete the addition.

Answer see page 243

160

PUZZLE 263

Which tile should replace the question mark? The top and bottom boxes may move independently of each other.

Answer see page 243

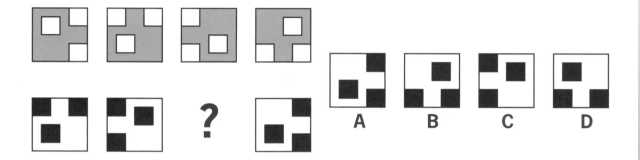

PUZZLE 264

Complete the analogy.

Answer see page 243

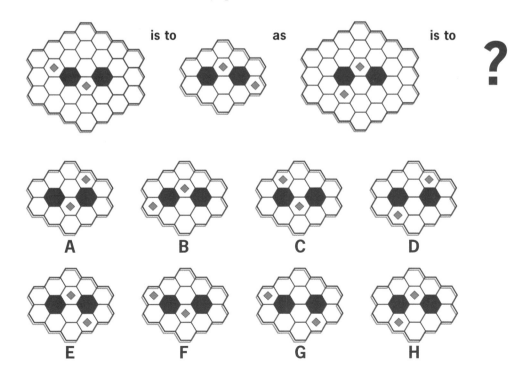

PUZZLE 265

Find the 8 differences in picture B.

Answer see page 243

A

B

PUZZLE 266

Find the two shapes that don't go with the other three.

Answer see page 243

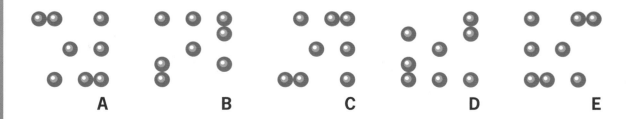

A   B   C   D   E

PUZZLE 267

This system is in balance. The black block weighs the same as the pale blocks. If three more blocks are placed on the black block, where should two pale blocks be placed to return the system to balance?

Answer see page 243

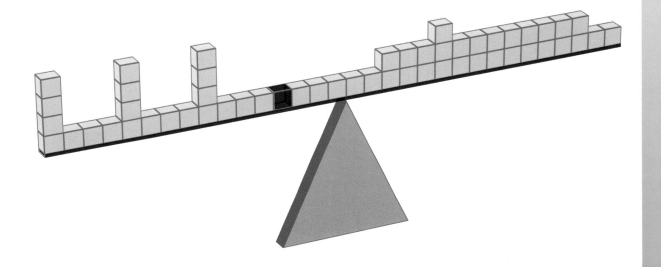

PUZZLE 268

Which of the following is the odd one out?

Answer see page 244

A

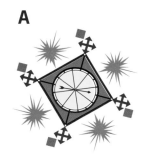

B

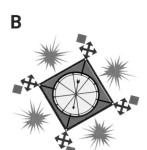

C

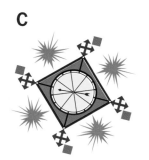

D

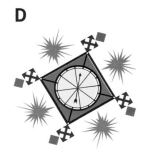

PUZZLE 269

Only two of these butterflies are identical. Which are they?

Answer see page 244

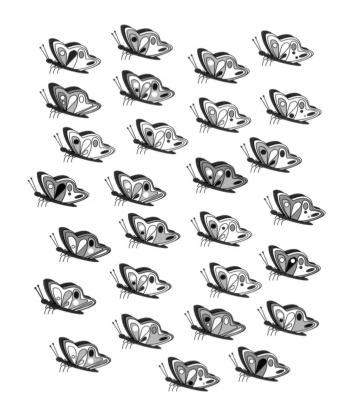

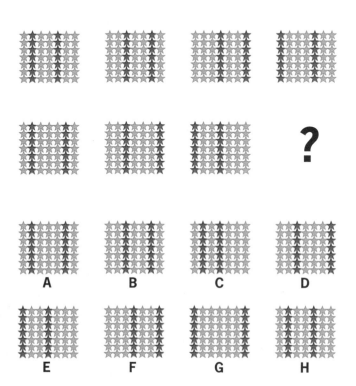

A   B   C   D

E   F   G   H

PUZZLE 270

Which is the missing panel?

Answer see page 244

PUZZLE 271

How many kangaroos are in this herd?

Answer see page 244

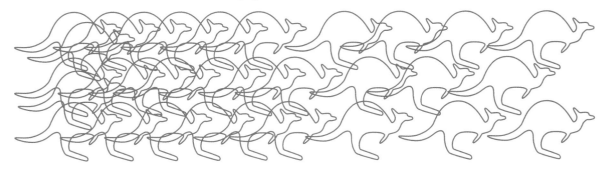

PUZZLE 272

Complete the analogy.

Answer see page 244

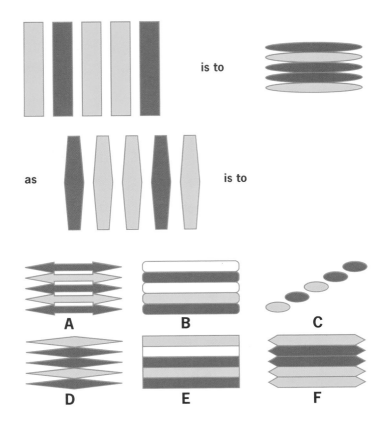

PUZZLE 273

Which two patterns do not go with the other three?

Answer see page 244

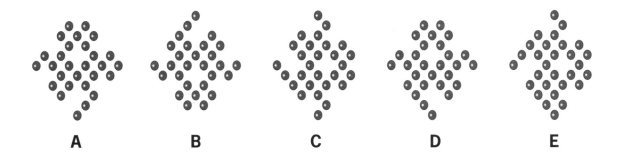

A   B   C   D   E

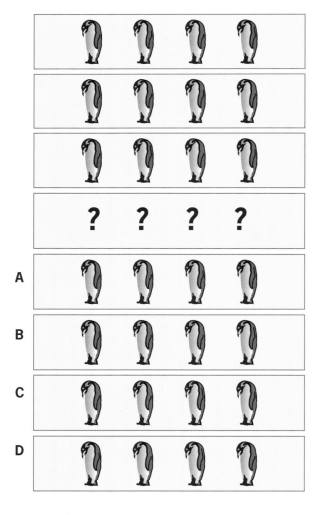

PUZZLE 274

Which tile comes next in this series?

Answer see page 244

PUZZLE 275

What comes next in this series?

Answer see page 244

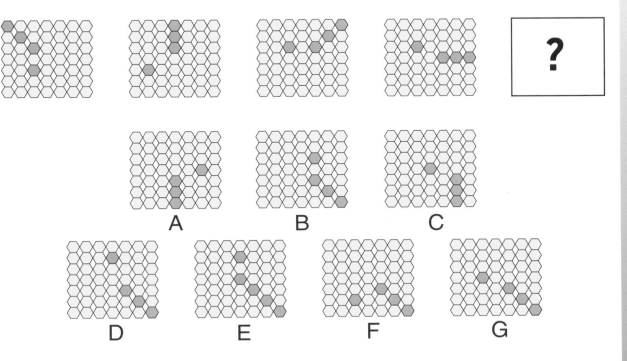

PUZZLE 276

If the wheel at A is turned as indicated, will the load first rise, or fall?

Answer see page 244

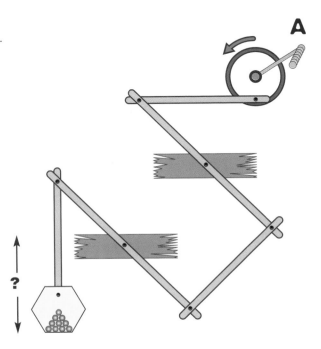

PUZZLE 277

Find a number to replace the question mark.

Answer see page 244

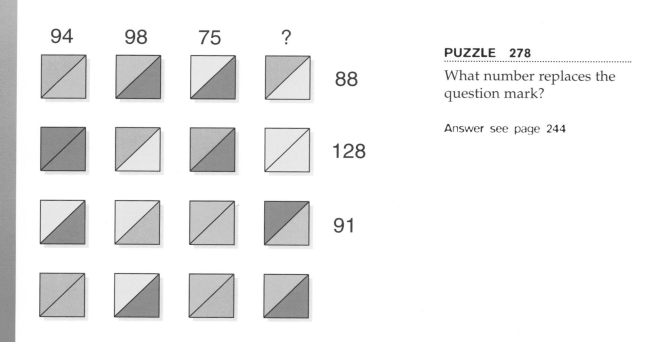

PUZZLE 278

What number replaces the question mark?

Answer see page 244

PUZZLE 279

What number replaces the question mark?

Answer see page 244

  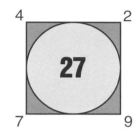 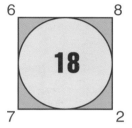

 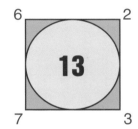 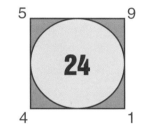 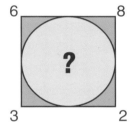

PUZZLE 280

What number replaces the question mark?

Answer see page 244

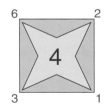   

   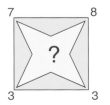

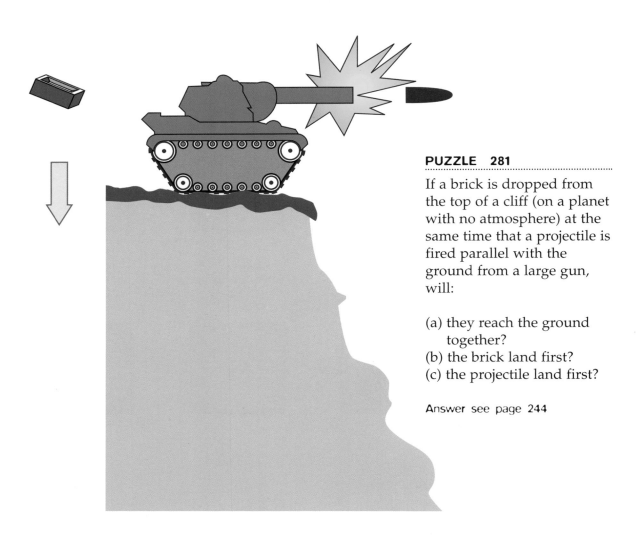

PUZZLE 281

If a brick is dropped from the top of a cliff (on a planet with no atmosphere) at the same time that a projectile is fired parallel with the ground from a large gun, will:

(a) they reach the ground together?
(b) the brick land first?
(c) the projectile land first?

Answer see page 244

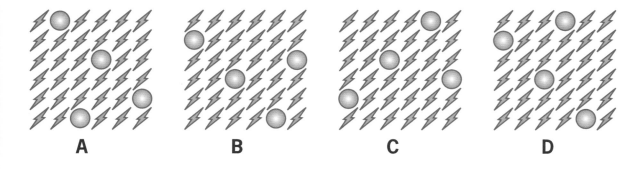

A   B   C   D

PUZZLE 282

Which of the following is the odd one out?

Answer see page 244

PUZZLE 283

The black dots represent hinge points. If points A and B are moved toward each other, will points C and D move together or apart?

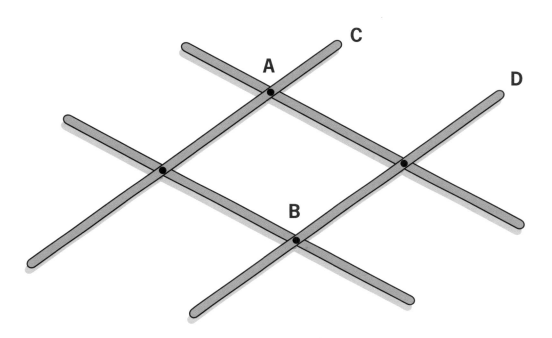

PUZZLE 284

Which of the following is the odd one out?

Answer see page 244

A　　　**B**　　　**C**　　　**D**

PUZZLE 285

Which of the following is the odd one out?

Answer see page 244

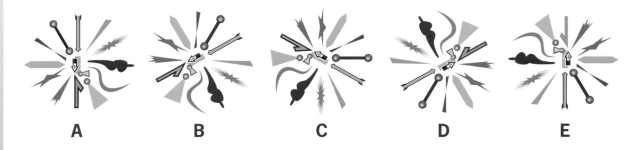

A   B   C   D   E

PUZZLE 286

Draw four straight lines that divide this puzzle into seven sections, with 3 pyramids and 7 balls in each section. The lines do not have to go from one edge to another.

Answer see page 245

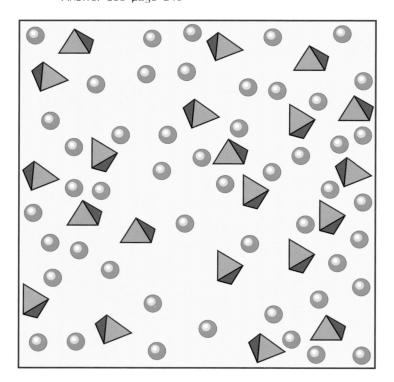

PUZZLE 287

Which set of shapes fits into the middle of
this panel to complete the pattern?

Answer see page 245

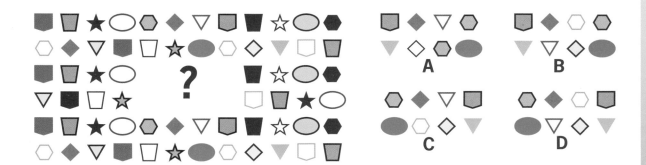

PUZZLE 288

Which of the following
make three pairs of identical
scenes?

Answer see page 245

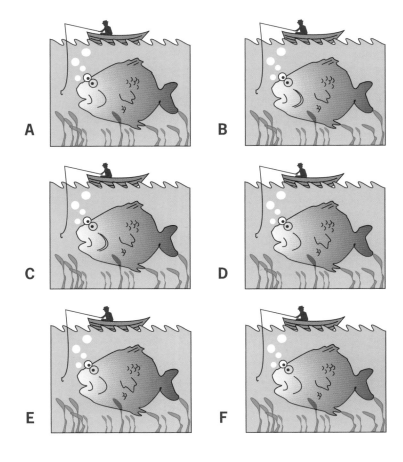

PUZZLE 289

Which of the following is the odd one out?

Answer see page 245

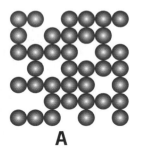 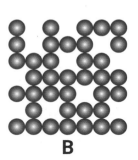  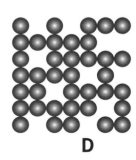

A   B   C   D

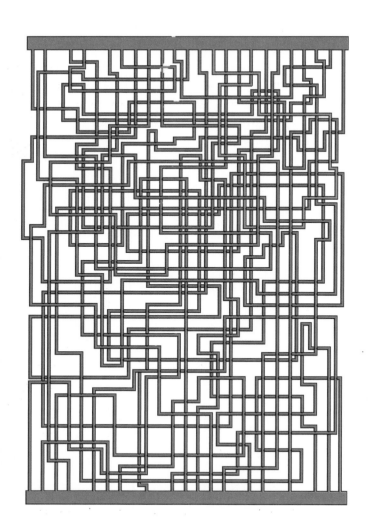

PUZZLE 290

Find the 8 places where the routes meet to form crossroads rather than crossovers.

Answer see page 245

PUZZLE 291

Here is a long multiplication sum. Each symbol represents a number from 0 to 9, and each like symbol always represents the same number. With this in mind, which symbol should replace the question mark?

Answer see page 245

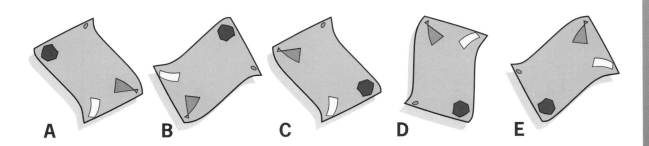

PUZZLE 292

Which of the following is the odd one out?

Answer see page 246

PUZZLE 293

What comes next in this series?

Answer see page 246

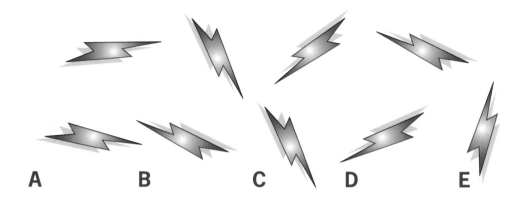

PUZZLE 294

Complete the analogy.

Answer see page 246

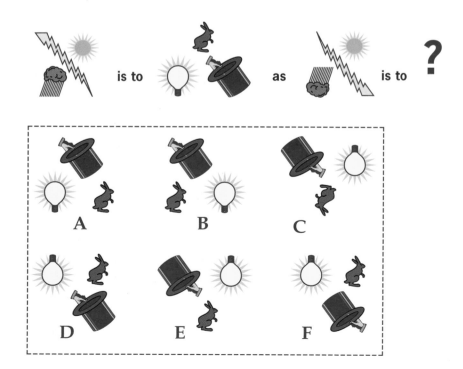

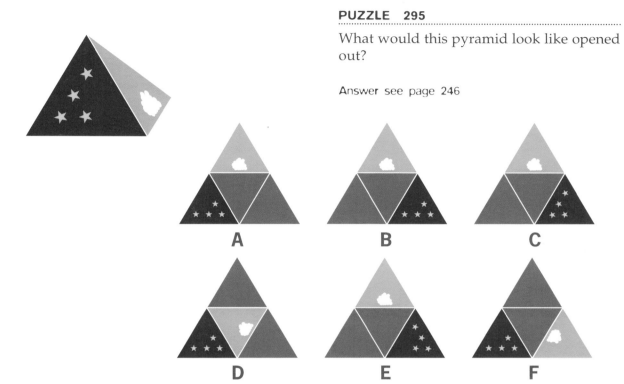

PUZZLE 295

What would this pyramid look like opened out?

Answer see page 246

PUZZLE 296

Which two of these form an identical pair that do not go with the other eight?

Answer see page 246

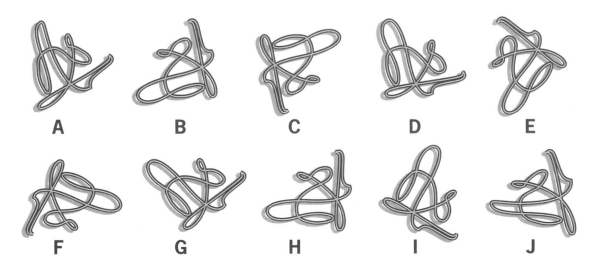

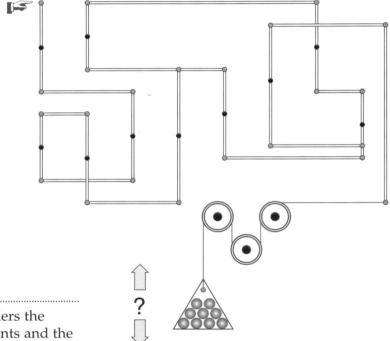

PUZZLE 297

In this system of levers and rollers the black spots are fixed swivel points and the shaded spots are non-fixed swivel points. With this in mind, if the lever is pushed as shown, will the load rise or fall?

Answer see page 246

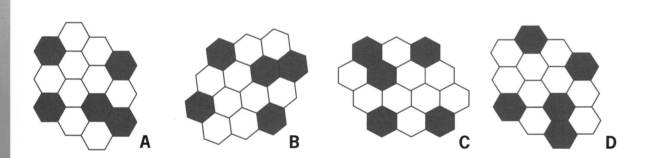

A   B   C   D

PUZZLE 298

Which of the above is the odd one out?

Answer see page 246

PUZZLE 299

From the information given, work out the missing total and the values of the different images.

Answer see page 246

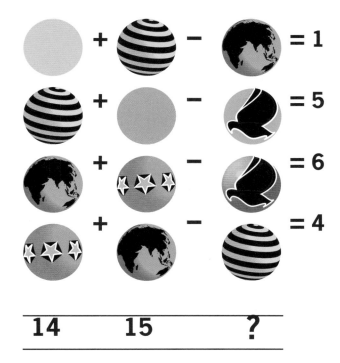

14   15   ?

PUZZLE 300

Which of the following is the odd one out?

Answer see page 246

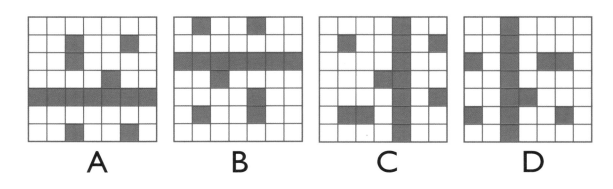

A   B   C   D

PUZZLE 301

What comes next in this series?

Answer see page 246

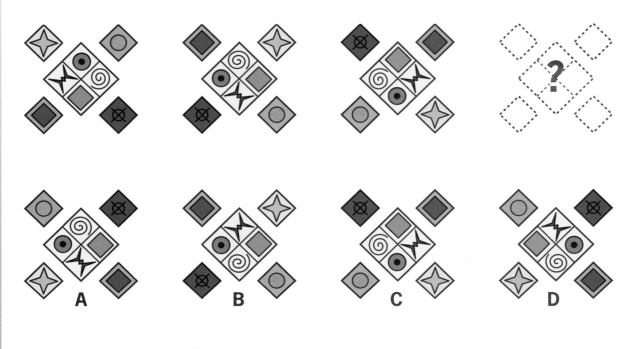

PUZZLE 302

Which figure or figures below is or are
identical to the one in the box?

Answer see page 246

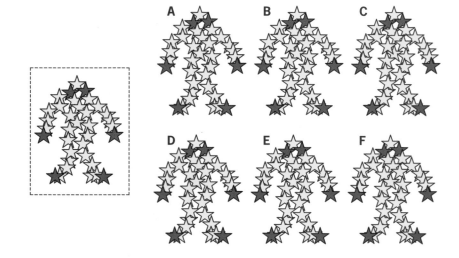

PUZZLE 303

Complete the analogy.

Answer see page 246

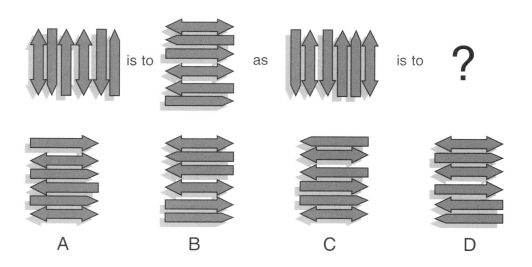

PUZZLE 304

Which pattern can be used to make the box in the middle?

Answer see page 246

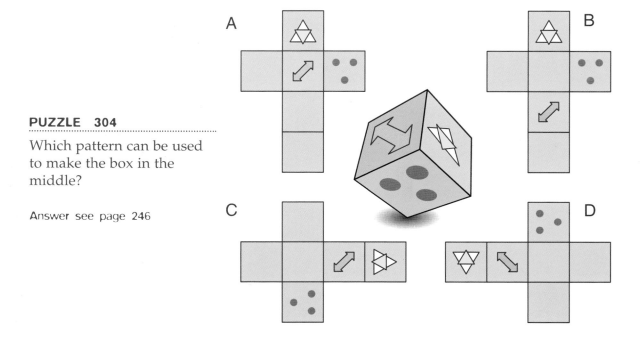

PUZZLE 305

Which of the following is the odd one out?

Answer see page 246

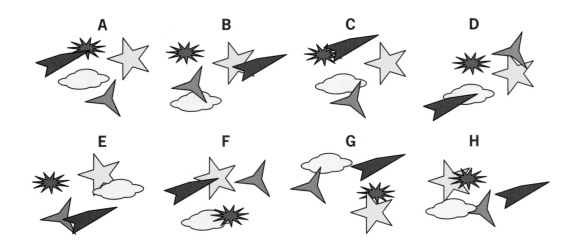

PUZZLE 306

Mark the 12 differences in picture B.

Answer see page 246

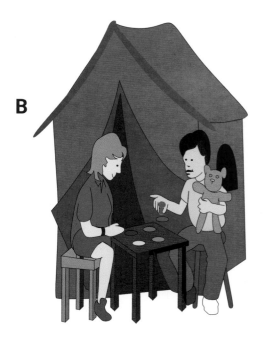

PUZZLE 307

What comes next in this series?

Answer see page 246

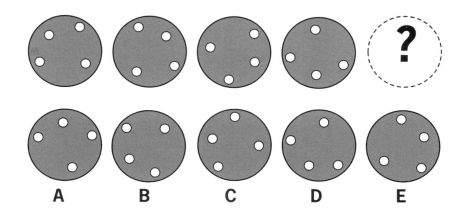

PUZZLE 308

What comes next in this series?

Answer see page 246

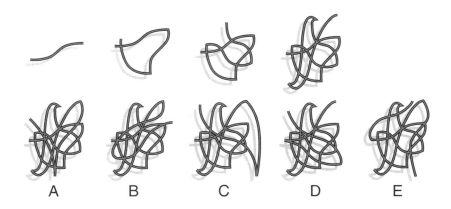

PUZZLE 309

Draw three straight lines that divide this puzzle into four sections, each with, respectively, 4, 5, 6 and 7 snakes, drums and clouds. The lines do not have to go from one edge to another.

Answer see page 246

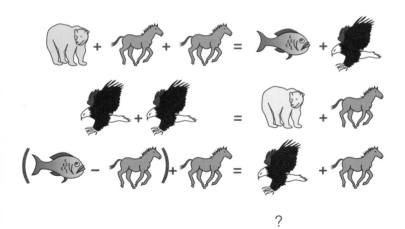

?

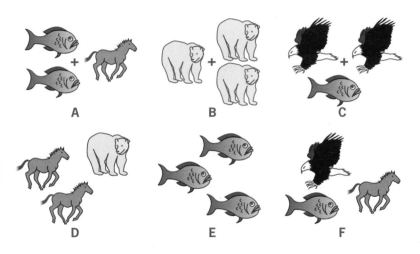

PUZZLE 310

Each like animal has the same value and the bear, horse, fish and bird all have different values. Which of A, B, C, D, E or F is the total value of the single column above the question mark, and what are the lowest possible values of the animals?

Answer see page 247

PUZZLE 311

As park ranger on this safari you have to collect as many rattlesnakes as possible without getting killed or maimed by them or other creatures. The wildcats will eat a part of your body if you step onto a sector which they have scent marked and the bears will hug you to death. The bears and wildcats have marked one segment next to the one they stand on, but you have no way of knowing which one. You may not go back over your tracks. Start on the shaded sector and finish on the snake facing the other way.

Answer see page 247

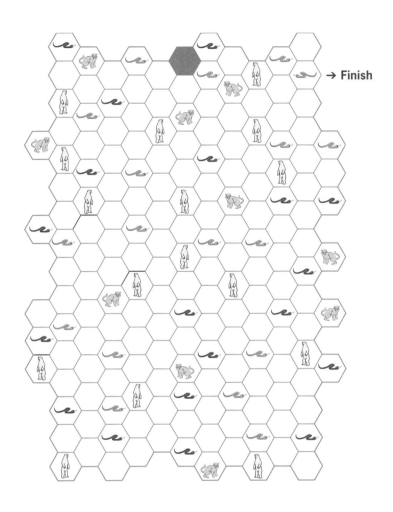

→ Finish

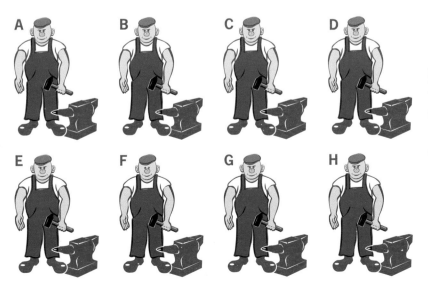

PUZZLE 312

Which of the following is the odd one out?

Answer see page 247

PUZZLE 313

Which one of these strings leads you to the diamond?

Answer see page 247

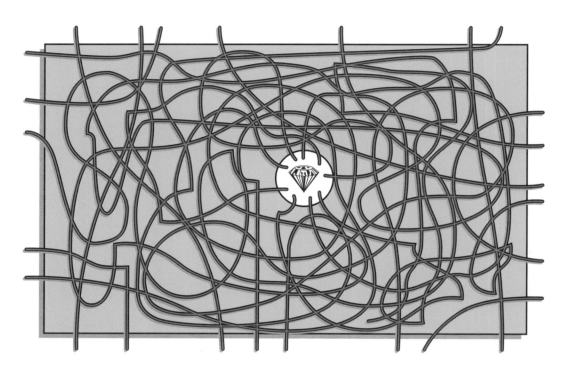

PUZZLE 314

Which of the following is the odd one out?

Answer see page 247

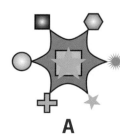
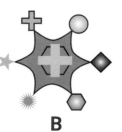
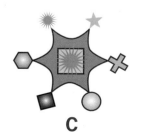
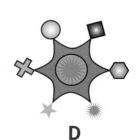

A   B   C   D

PUZZLE 315

Which tile is missing from the following panel?

Answer see page 247

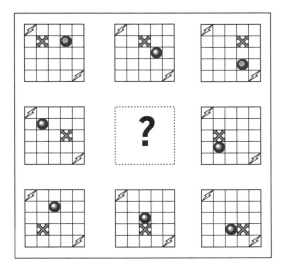

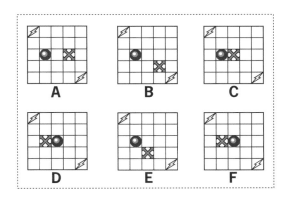

PUZZLE 316

Which set does not go with the other three?

Answer see page 247

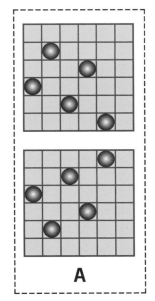

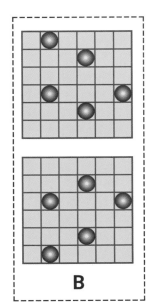

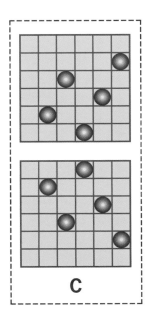

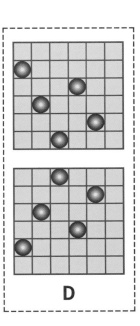

PUZZLE 317

What comes next in this series?

Answer see page 247

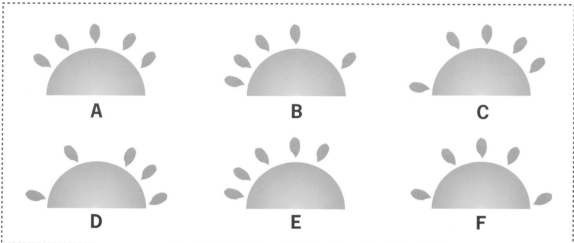

PUZZLE 318

What comes next in this series?

Answer see page 247

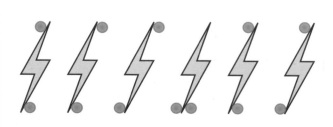
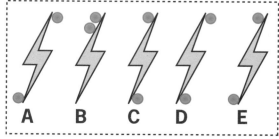

PUZZLE 319

Which of the following is the odd one out?

Answer see page 247

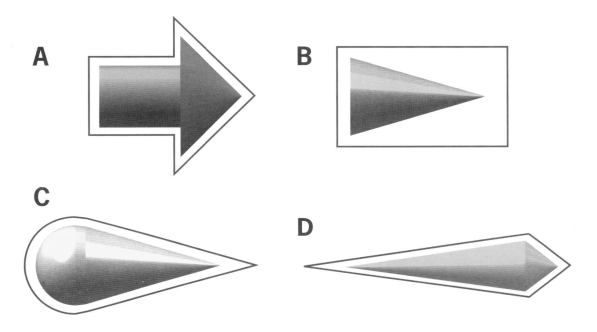

PUZZLE 320

Which of the following is the odd one out?

Answer see page 247

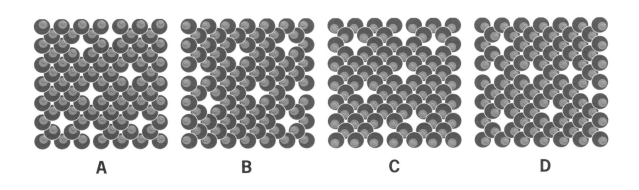

PUZZLE 321

What number replaces the question mark?

Answer see page 248

  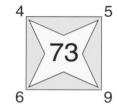 

 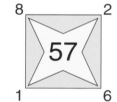  

PUZZLE 322

What letters replace the question mark?

Answer see page 248

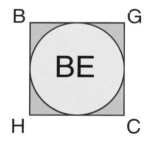 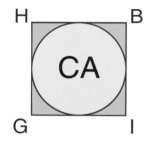 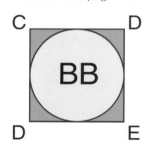 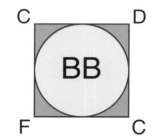

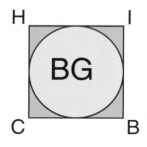 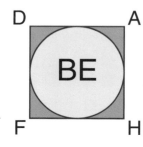 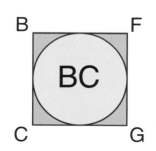 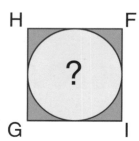

PUZZLE 323

What pairs of letters replace the question marks?

Answer see page 248

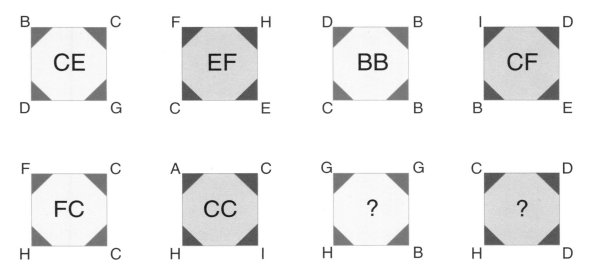

PUZZLE 324

What number replaces the question mark?

Answer see page 248

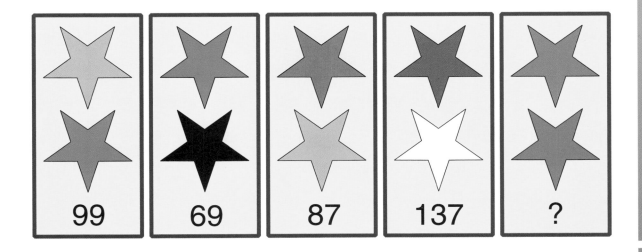

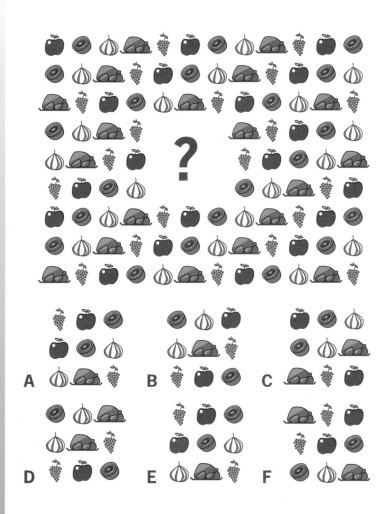

PUZZLE 325

Which set should the replace the question mark to complete the pattern?

Answer see page 248

PUZZLE 326

Which of the following is the odd one out?

Answer see page 248

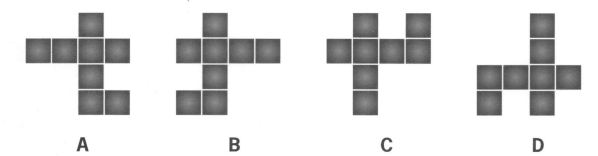

A   B   C   D

PUZZLE 327

Which set of tiles goes into the middle to complete the pattern?

Answer see page 248

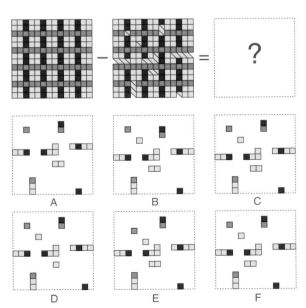

PUZZLE 328

Which panel should replace the question mark?

Answer see page 248

MENSA MENSA MENSA MENSA MENSA MENSA MENSA MENSA

PUZZLE 329

Which of the following is the odd one out?

Answer see page 248

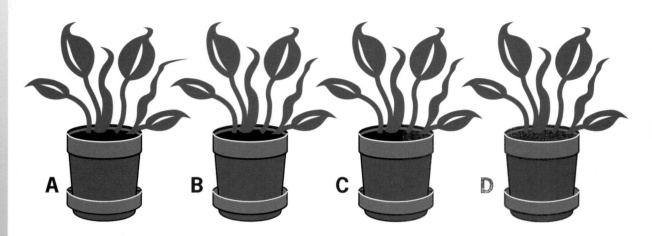

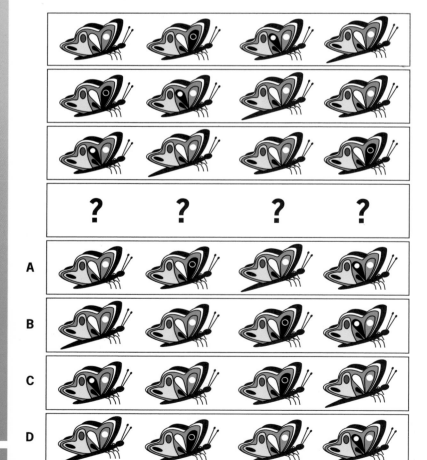

PUZZLE 330

Which tile comes next in this series?

Answer see page 248

194

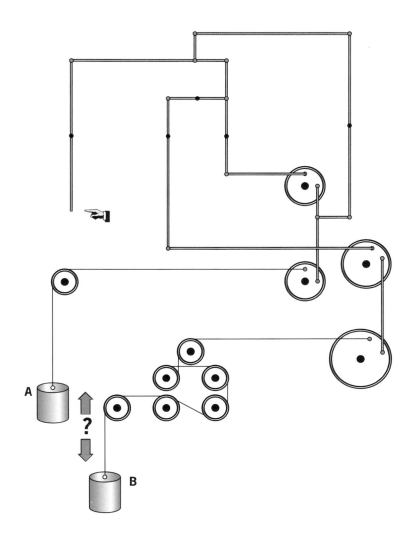

PUZZLE 331

In this system of levers and rollers, in which the shaded spots are non-fixed swivel points and the black spots are fixed swivel points, if the lever is pushed as shown, will each load at A and B rise or fall?

Answer see page 248

PUZZLE 332

Which of the following is the odd one out?

Answer see page 248

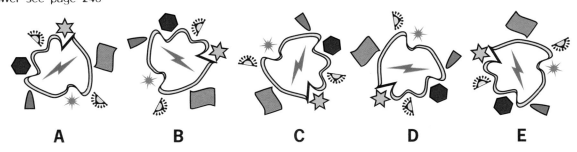

A   **B**   **C**   **D**   **E**

PUZZLE 333

Draw three straight lines that divide this puzzle into six sections that contain 1 fish and 1 flag in each and respectively 0, 1, 2, 3, 4 and 5 drums and lightning bolts. The lines do not have to go from one edge to another.

Answer see page 248

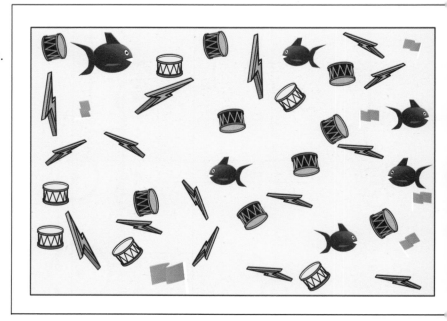

PUZZLE 334

The symbols in the following calculations represent the numbers from 0 to 9. Each like symbol always represents the same number. What symbol should replace the question mark?

Answer see page 248

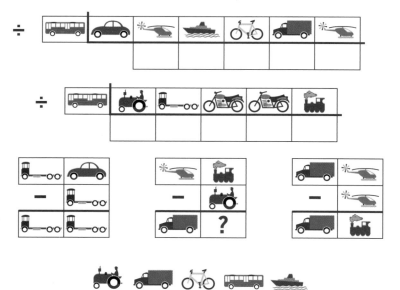

PUZZLE 335

What should replace the
question mark?

Answer see page 249

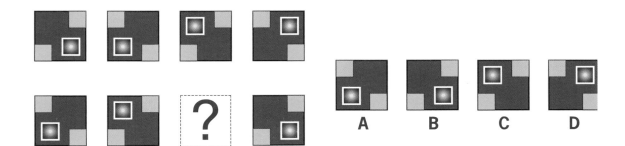

PUZZLE 336

What will happen when the
pedal turns?

Answer see page 249

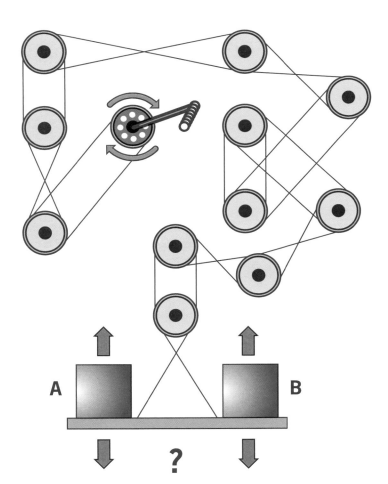

PUZZLE 337

What comes next?

Answer see page 249

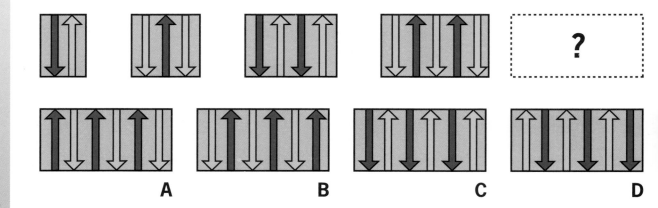

PUZZLE 338

What comes next in this series?

Answer see page 249

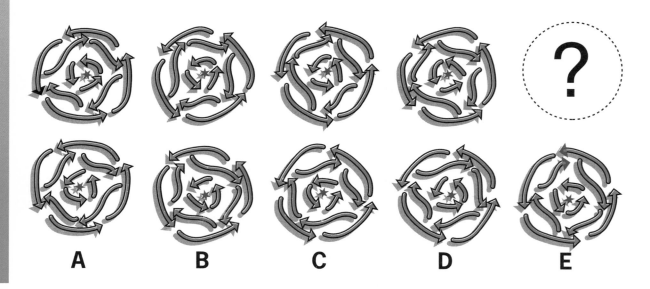

PUZZLE 339

Complete the analogy.

Answer see page 249

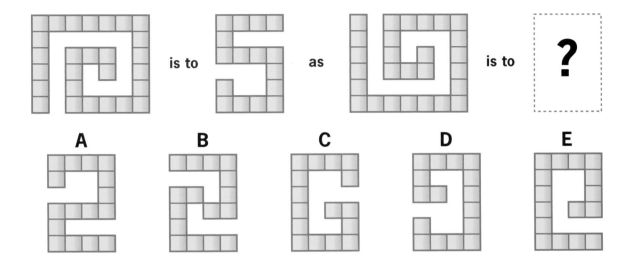

PUZZLE 340

Which of the following is the odd one out?

Answer see page 249

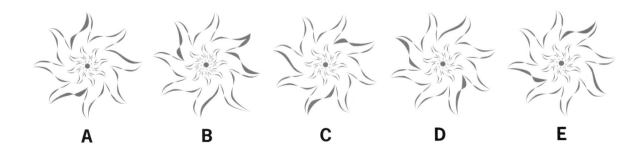

PUZZLE 341

Find the 14 differences in picture B.

Answer see page 249

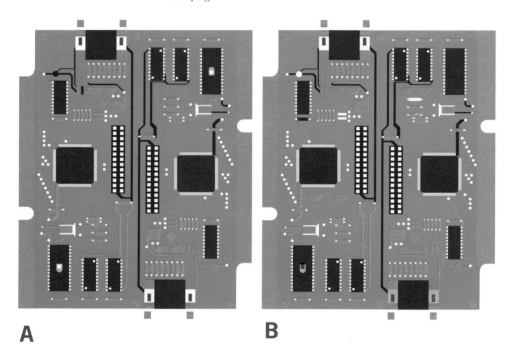

A
B

PUZZLE 342

What should replace the question mark?

Answer see page 249

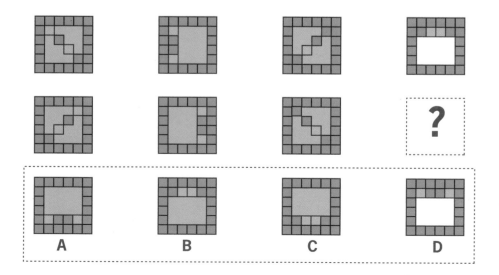

A
B
C
D

PUZZLE 343

Find the only continuous route from the left of this puzzle to the right.

Answer see page 249

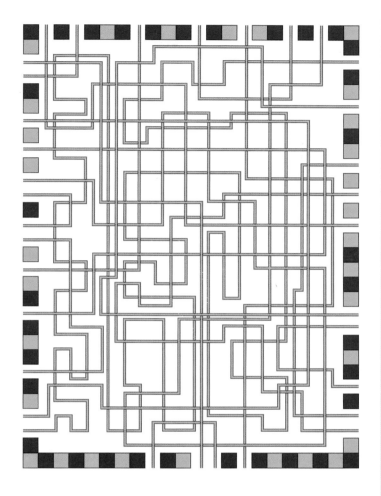

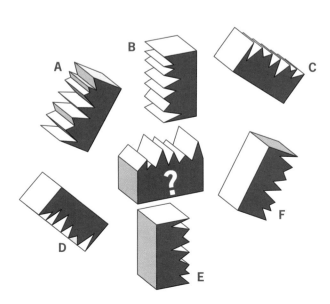

PUZZLE 344

Which of the surrounding pieces fits perfectly on top of the middle piece to make a rectangular block?

Answer see page 250

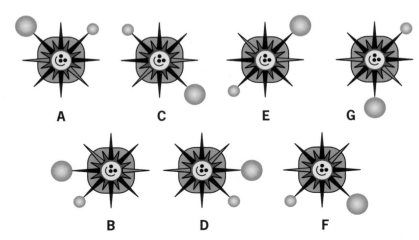

A   **C**   **E**   **G**

B   **D**   **F**

PUZZLE 345

Which of the following is the odd one out?

Answer see page 250

PUZZLE 346

Which objects should replace the question marks?

Answer see page 250

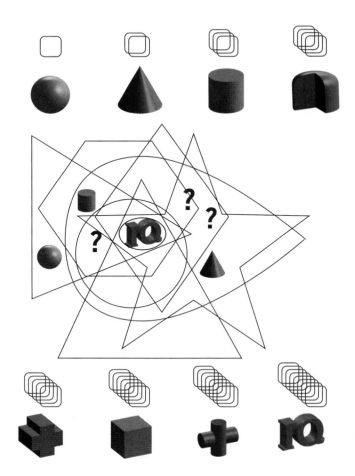

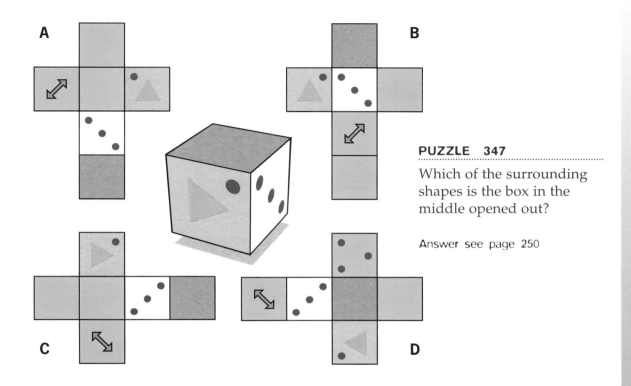

PUZZLE 347

Which of the surrounding shapes is the box in the middle opened out?

Answer see page 250

PUZZLE 348

Complete the analogy.

Answer see page 250

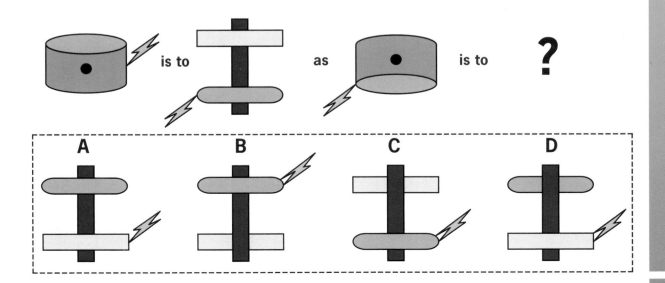

203

PUZZLE 349

Which is the odd one out?

Answer see page 250

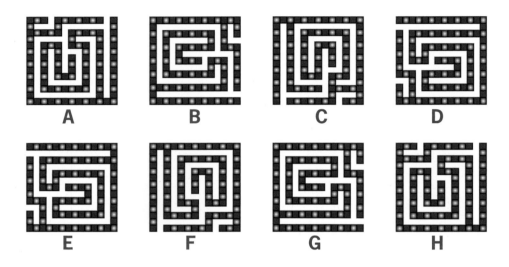

PUZZLE 350

In this system of pulley wheels and levers, where the black spots are fixed pivots and the shaded spots are non-fixed pivots, will (A) rise or fall and will (B) rise or fall when the wheel at the top is turned in the direction indicated?

Answer see page 250

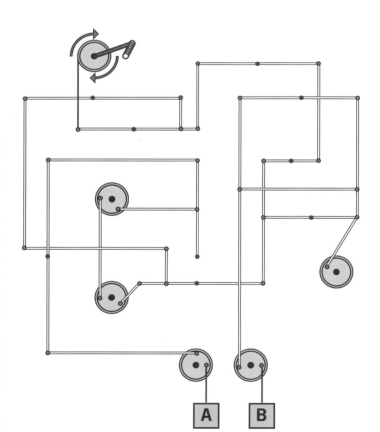

PUZZLE 351

Which of the figures below
is the same as the one in the
box?

Answer see page 250

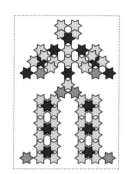

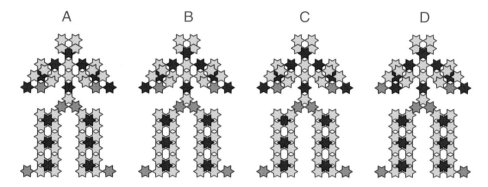

A B C D

PUZZLE 352

Which of the following is the odd one out?

Answer see page 250

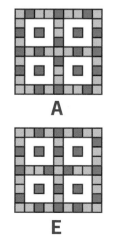

A

B

C

D

E

F

G

H

PUZZLE 353

Draw five straight lines that divide this puzzle into six sections that have 1 chimp, 1 koala, 3 snakes, 4 dogs and 5 stars in each section. The lines do not have to go from one edge to another.

Answer see page 250

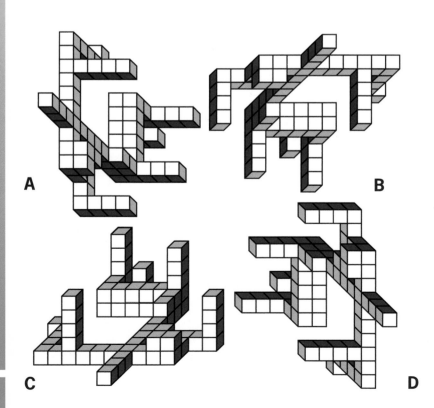

A

B

C

D

PUZZLE 354

Which of the four is the odd one out?

Answer see page 250

PUZZLE 355

Which of the figures below should replace the question mark in the box?

Answer see page 250

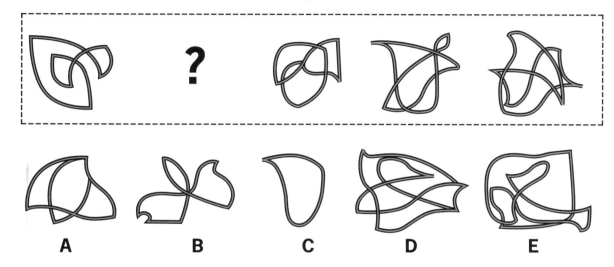

A   B   C   D   E

PUZZLE 356

Complete the analogy.

Answer see page 250

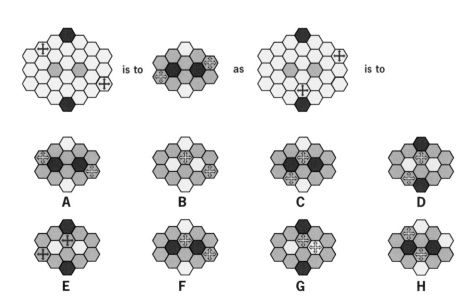

PUZZLE 357

A blue block below weighs three times a pink block. Where should one blue block be placed to return this system to balance?

Answer see page 250

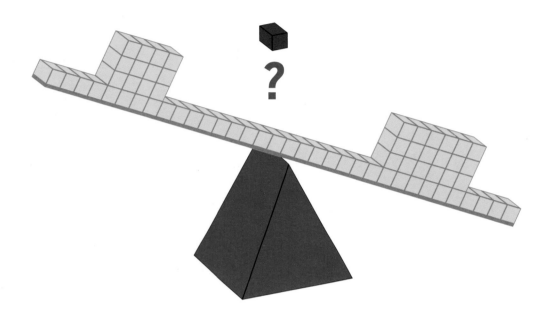

PUZZLE 358

Which of the following is the odd one out?

Answer see page 250

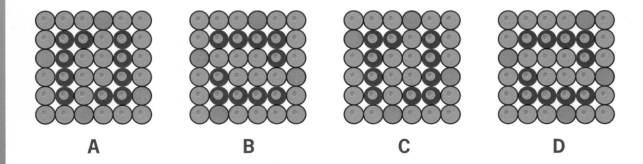

A   B   C   D

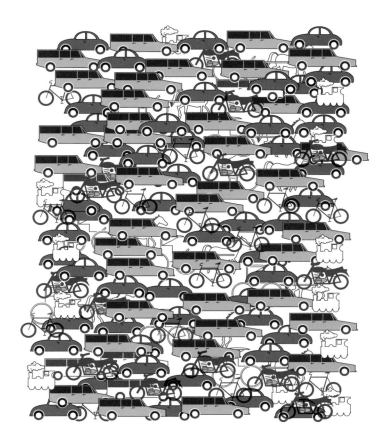

PUZZLE 359

Find the 10 horse & carriage sets hidden behind these vehicles.

Answer see page 251

A

B

C

D

PUZZLE 360

Which of these is the odd one out?

Answer see page 251

PUZZLE 361

What comes next in this series?

Answer see page 251

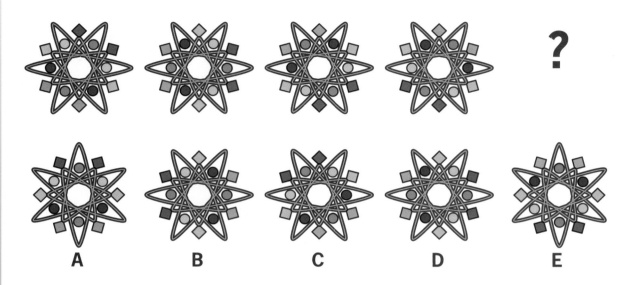

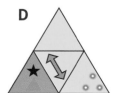
A

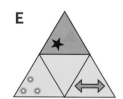
B

C

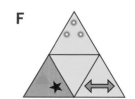
D

E

PUZZLE 362

What would this pyramid look like opened out?

Answer see page 251

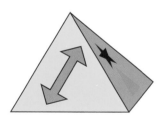

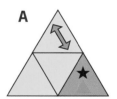
A   B   C

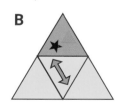

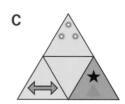
D   E   F

PUZZLE 363

In this system of cogs, levers and pulley wheels, in which the black spots are fixed pivot points and the shaded spots are non-fixed pivot points, the loads at A and B are in balance. Which one will rise when the wheel at the bottom is turned as indicated?

Answer see page 251

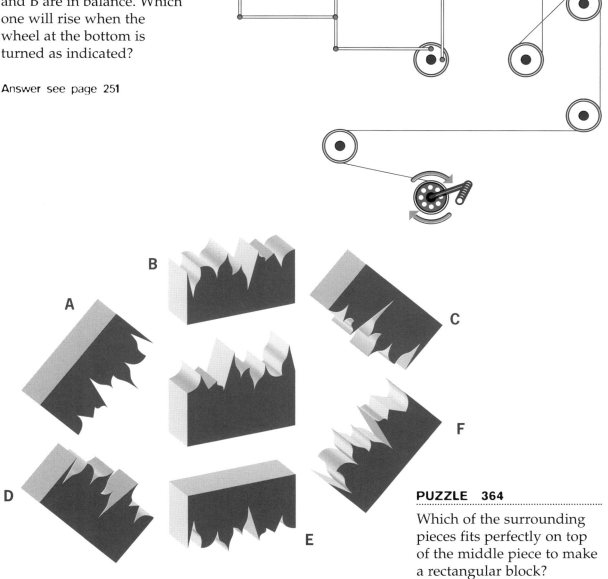

PUZZLE 364

Which of the surrounding pieces fits perfectly on top of the middle piece to make a rectangular block?

Answer see page 251

PUZZLE 365

What number replaces the question mark?

Answer see page 251

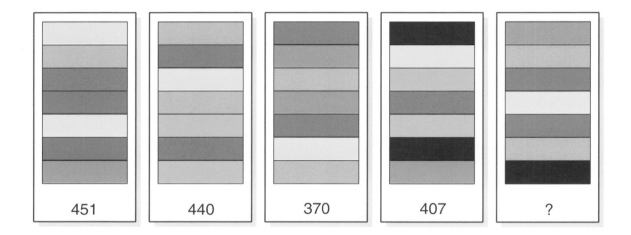

451   440   370   407   ?

PUZZLE 366

What number replaces the question mark?

Answer see page 251

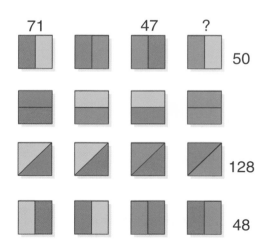

PUZZLE 367

What number replaces the question mark?

Answer see page 251

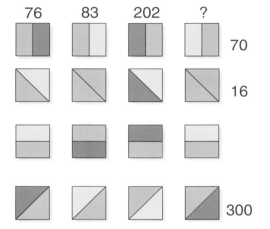

PUZZLE 368

What is blue worth?

Answer see page 251

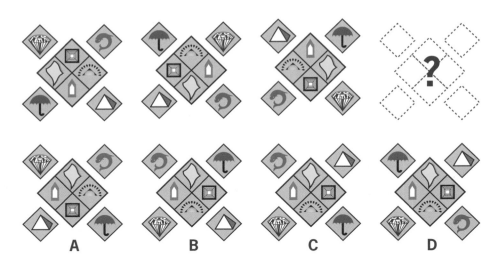

PUZZLE 369

What comes next in this series?

Answer see page 251

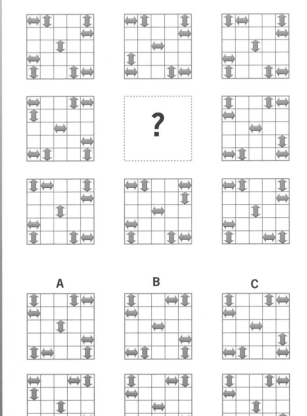

PUZZLE 370

Which tile is missing from this series of panels?

Answer see page 251

PUZZLE 371

Which of the following is the odd one out?

Answer see page 251

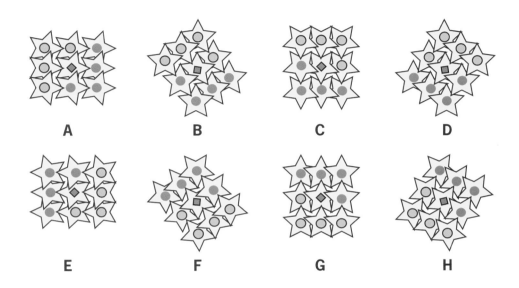

PUZZLE 372

Which two of these images are identical?

Answer see page 251

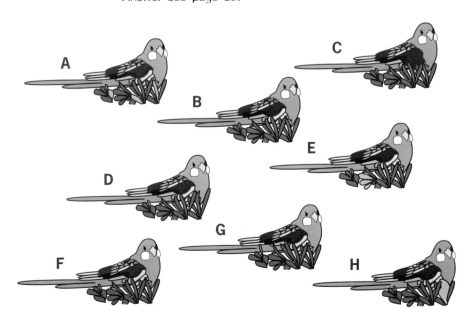

PUZZLE 373

Find the 14 differences in picture B.

Answer see page 251

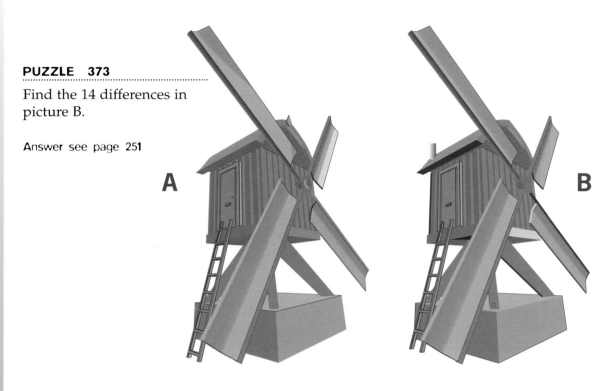

PUZZLE 374

Which is the missing set?

Answer see page 251

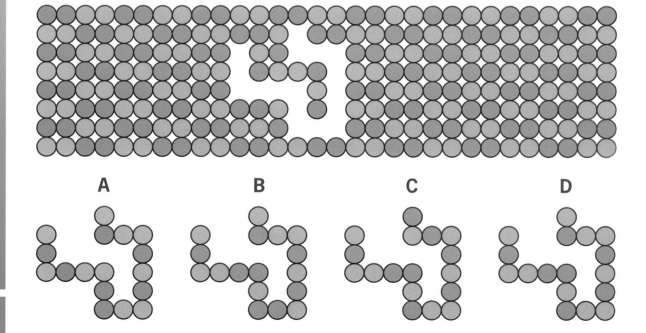

A   B   C   D

PUZZLE 375

Map out the route to the diamond using the key on the right. Follow the direction of the apex of the triangle; for example the triangle to the right of Start is pointing right, so you should go 6 squares right. You may travel forward, back, up or down, but not diagonally nor retrace your steps, although your path may criss-cross.

Answer see page 252

PUZZLE 376

Draw three lines that connect the next three drums in sequence with the boxes they should go in.

Answer see page 252

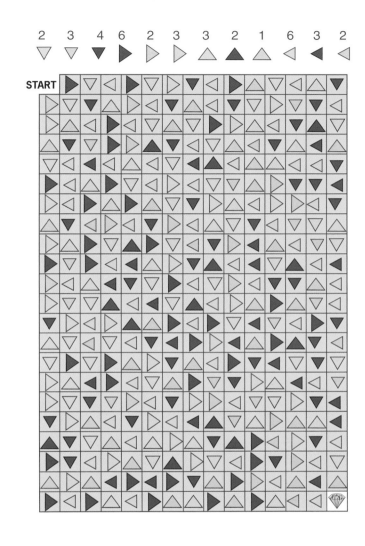

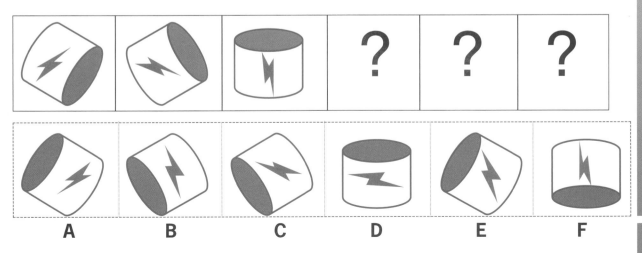

A   B   C   D   E   F

PUZZLE 377

Which of the following is the odd one out?

Answer see page 252

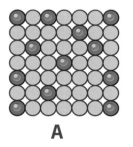

A

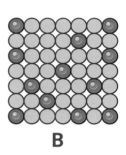

B

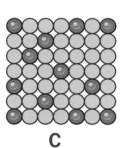

C

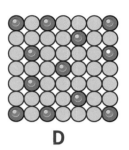

D

PUZZLE 378

Complete the analogy.

Answer see page 252

 is to 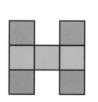 as  is to

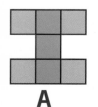

A

B

C

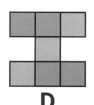

D

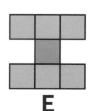

E

PUZZLE 379

What comes next in this series?

Answer see page 252

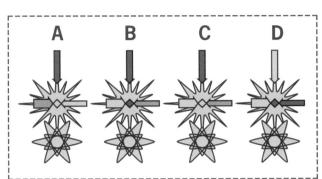

PUZZLE 380

Which is the missing set?

Answer see page 252

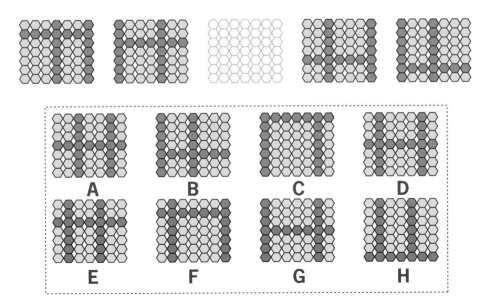

PUZZLE 381

How many cobras are in this menacing group?

Answer see page 252

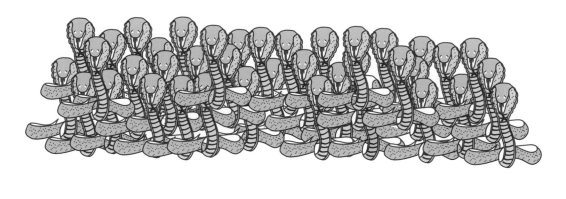

PUZZLE 382

Draw three straight lines that make four sections with a total value of 40 in each, using the values given above. The lines do not have to go from one edge to another.

Answer see page 252

PUZZLE 383

Which of the following is the odd one out?

Answer see page 252

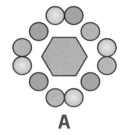 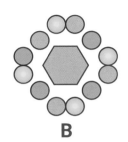 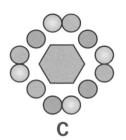 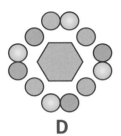

A   B   C   D

PUZZLE 384

Which of the following is the odd one out?

Answer see page 252

A   B   C   D

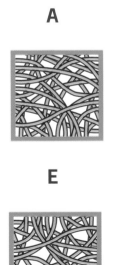 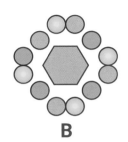 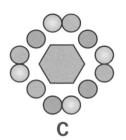 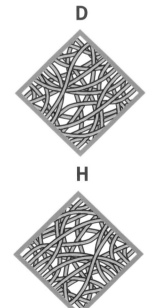

E   F   G   H

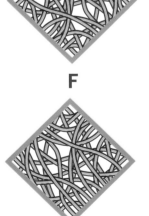 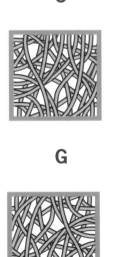

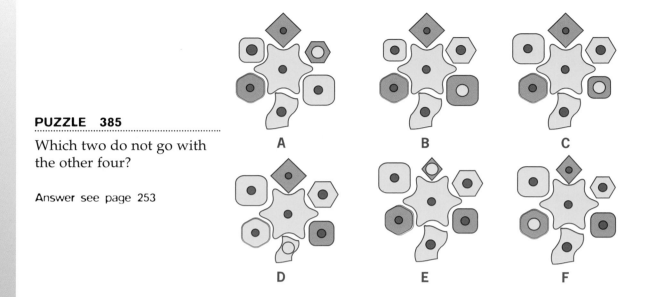

PUZZLE 385

Which two do not go with the other four?

Answer see page 253

A   B   C

D   E   F

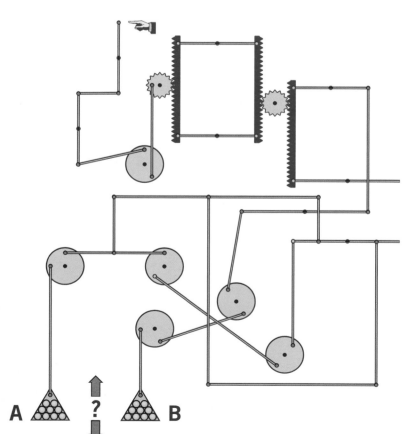

A   ?   B

PUZZLE 386

In this system of cogs, levers and rollers, in which the black spots are fixed swivel points and the shaded spots are non-fixed swivel points, does the load at A and the load at B rise or drop when the lever at the top is pushed as shown?

Answer see page 253

PUZZLE 387

Each like animal has the same value and the leopard, flea, dog and rabbit all have different values. Which of A, B, C, D, E or F is the total value of the single column above the question mark, and what are the lowest possible values of the animals?

Answer see page 252

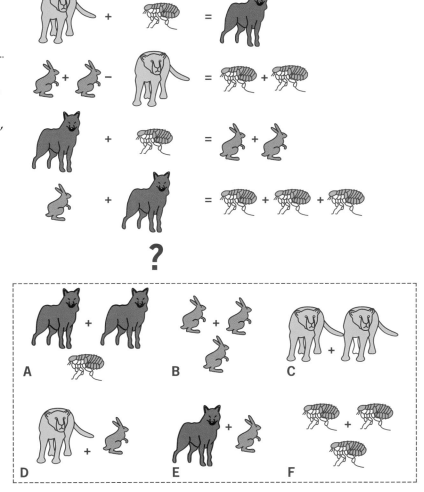

PUZZLE 388

Which of the following is the odd one out?

Answer see page 252

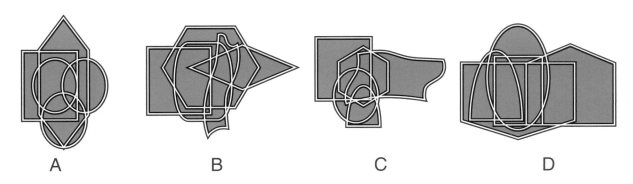

A   B   C   D

A

PUZZLE 389

What are the 15 differences in picture B?

Answer see page 253

B

PUZZLE 390

Complete the analogy.

Answer see page 253

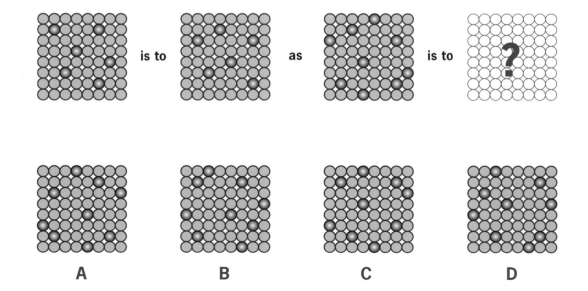

A   B   C   D

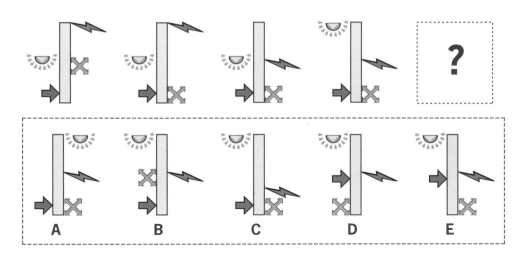

PUZZLE 391

Which comes next in this series?

Answer see page 253

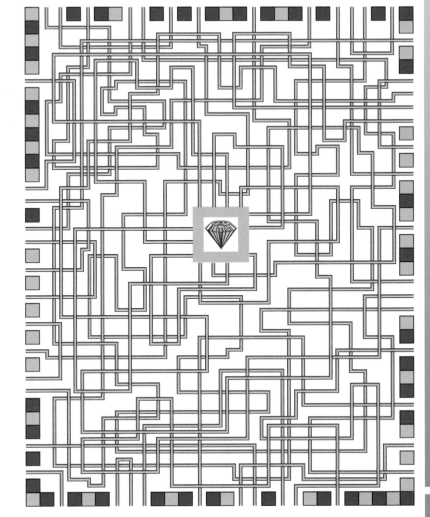

PUZZLE 392

Find the only route from the perimeter of this field to the shaded path around the diamond.

Answer see page 253

225

PUZZLE 393

Find the odd one out in each row.

Answer see page 253

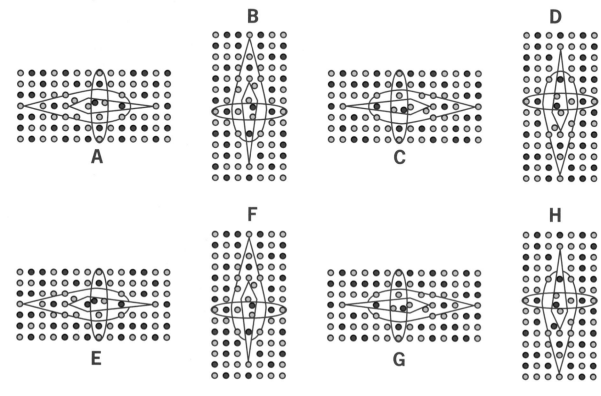

PUZZLE 394

Which of the following is the odd one out?

Answer see page 253

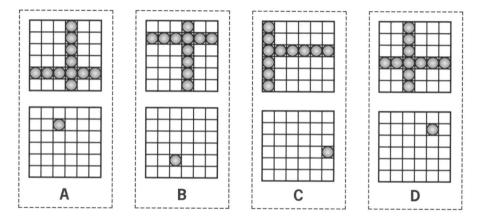

PUZZLE 395

Which is the missing panel?

Answer see page 253

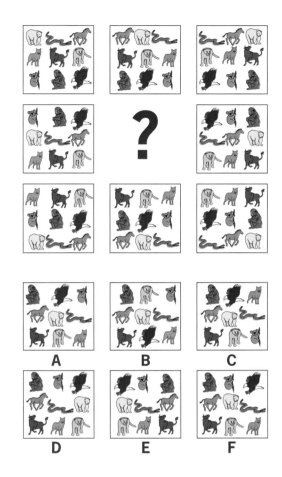

PUZZLE 396

Which of the following is the odd one out?

Answer see page 253

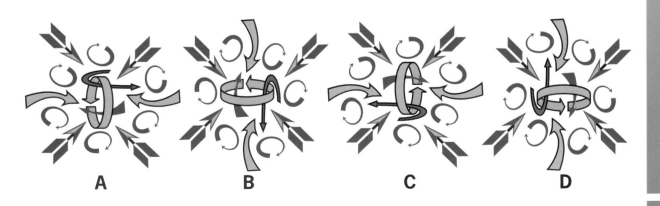

A B

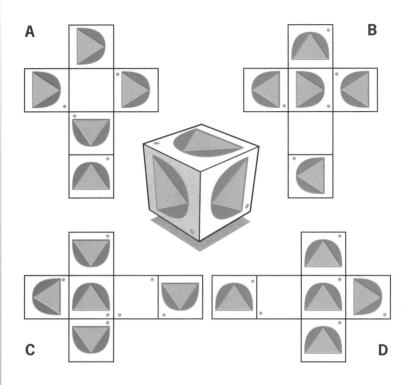

C D

PUZZLE 397

When the cube in the middle is opened out, which of the surrounding shapes does it make?

Answer see page 254

PUZZLE 398

Complete the analogy.

Answer see page 254

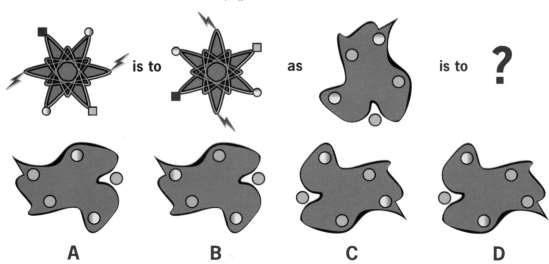

A   B   C   D

PUZZLE 399

Which of the surrounding shapes fits
exactly onto the middle piece to make a
rectangular block?

Answer see page 254

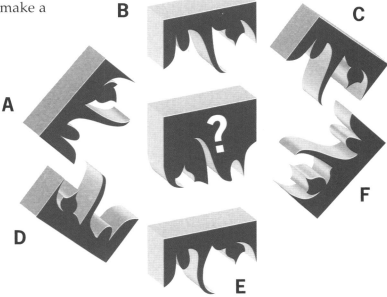

PUZZLE 400

Which clock is the odd-one-out?

Answer see page 254

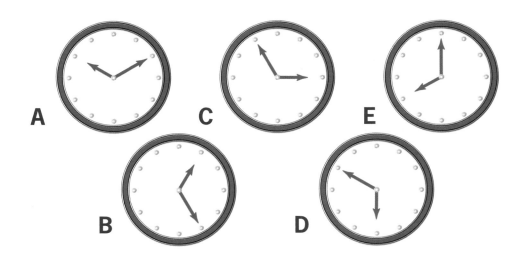

PUZZLE 401

Which of the following is the odd one out?

Answer see page 254

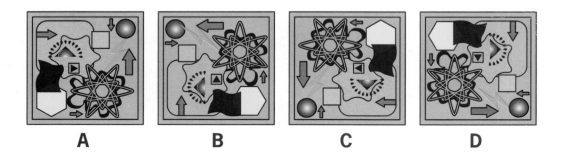

PUZZLE 402

Which jet fighter is missing?

Answer see page 254

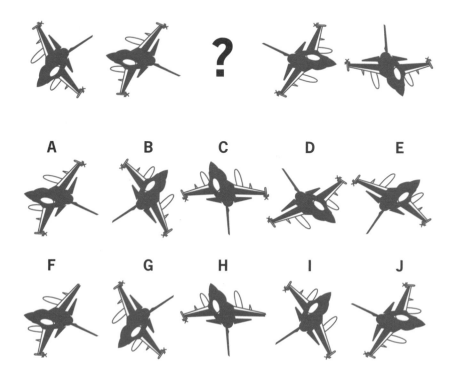

PUZZLE 403

Which of the following is the odd one out?

Answer see page 254

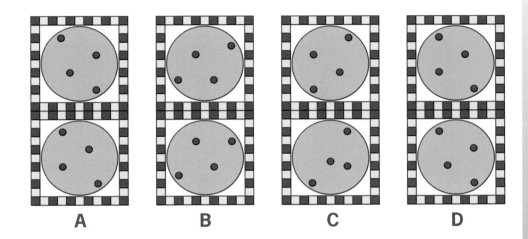

PUZZLE 404

Which panel should replace the question mark?

Answer see page 254

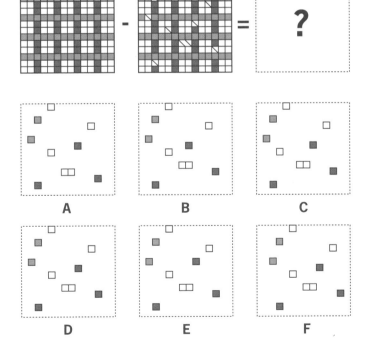

PUZZLE 405

Which of the following is the odd one out?

Answer see page 254

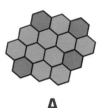  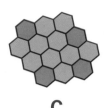  

A   **B**   **C**   **D**   **E**

PUZZLE 406

Draw four straight lines that divide this puzzle into five sections with 1 scuba diver, 3 fish and respectively, 4, 5, 6, 7 and 8 large bubbles and sea shells in each section. The lines do not have to go from one edge to another.

Answer see page 254

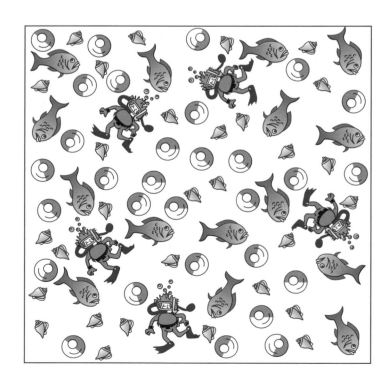

PUZZLE 407

Which of the following is the odd one out?

Answer see page 254

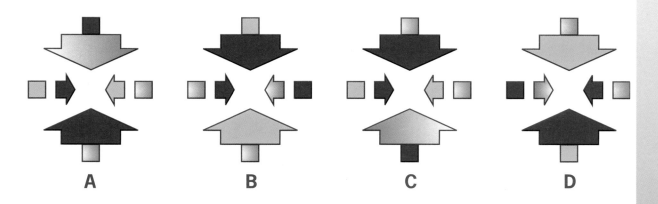

A   B   C   D

PUZZLE 408

Which is the odd one out in each row?

Answer see page 254

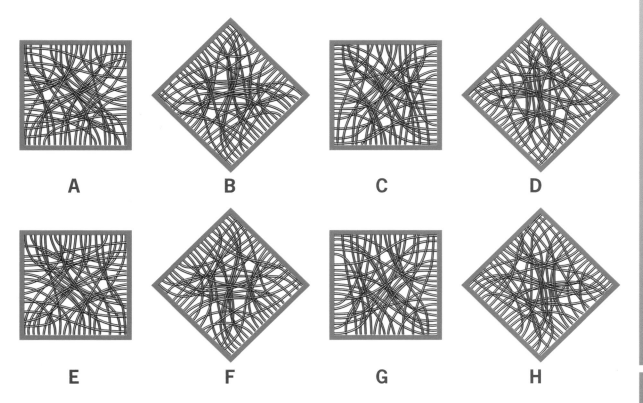

A   B   C   D

E   F   G   H

PUZZLE 409

What is pink worth?

Answer see page 254

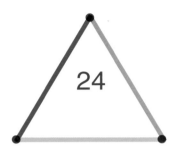 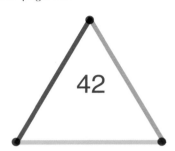 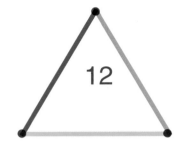

PUZZLE 410

What number could replace the question mark?

Answer see page 254

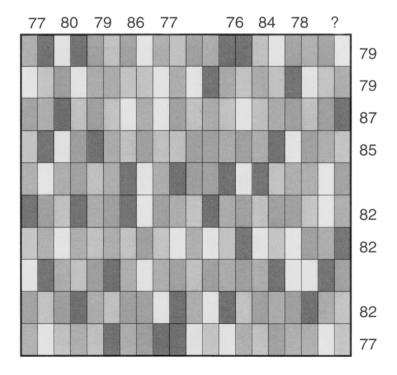

16 17   13 19 15   13 13 ?

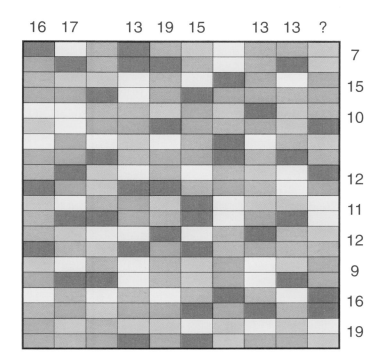

7

15

10

12

11

12

9

16

19

PUZZLE 411

What number could replace
the question mark?

Answer see page 254

258 269 212   237 217 254 268 242 ?

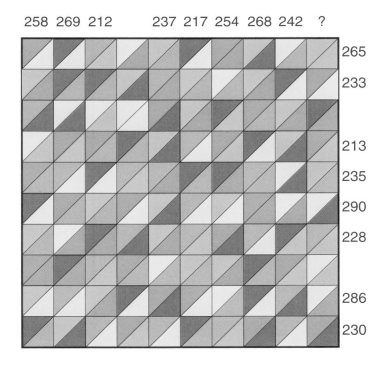

265

233

213

235

290

228

286

230

PUZZLE 412

What number could replace
the question mark?

Answer see page 254

PUZZLE 413

Which set fits into the middle of this set of tiles?

Answer see page 254

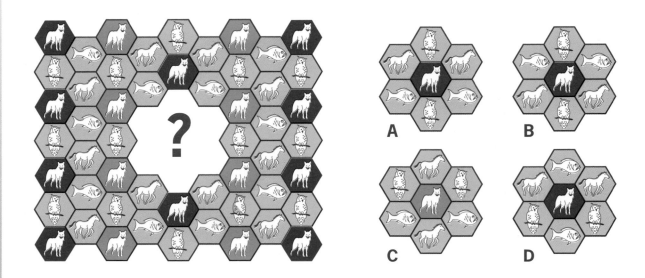

PUZZLE 414

These ramps are fixed in position. When the ball at the top is released, where will it eventually come to rest?

Answer see page 254

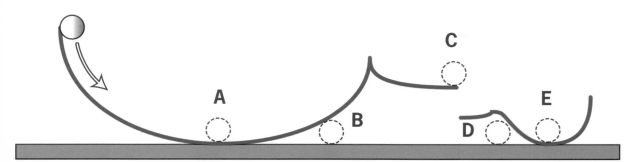

PUZZLE 415

This system is in balance. The load at B is on a plank which sits on top of two rollers. The black spots are fixed pivot points and the shaded spots are non-fixed pivot points. When the lever at the bottom is pushed as shown, will the load at A rise or fall and will the load at B move left or right?

Answer see page 254

PUZZLE 416

Complete the analogy.

Answer see page 255

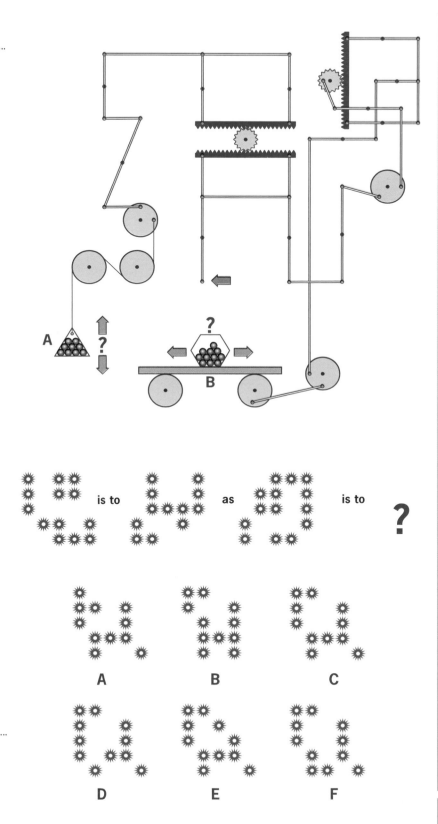

A   B   C

D   E   F

PUZZLE 417

Which comes next in this series?

Answer see page 255

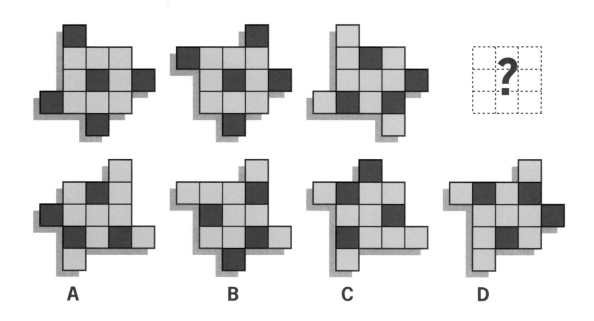

A   **B**   **C**   **D**

PUZZLE 418

Which of the following is the odd one out?

Answer see page 255

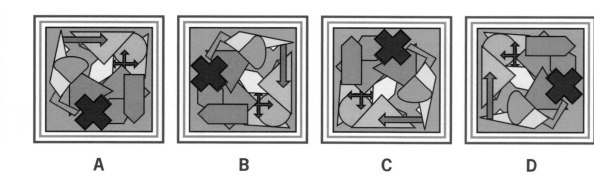

A   **B**   **C**   **D**

PUZZLE 419

Each like symbol has the same value throughout. What is the missing symbol? Clue: the small numbers are the totals for each row.

Answer see page 255

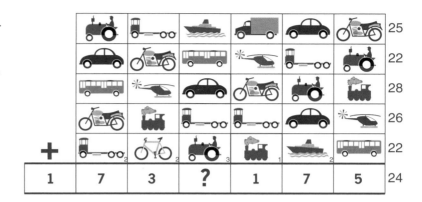

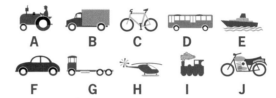

PUZZLE 420

Find the 18 differences in picture B.

Answer see page 255

PUZZLE 421

Which of the following is the odd one out?

Answer see page 255

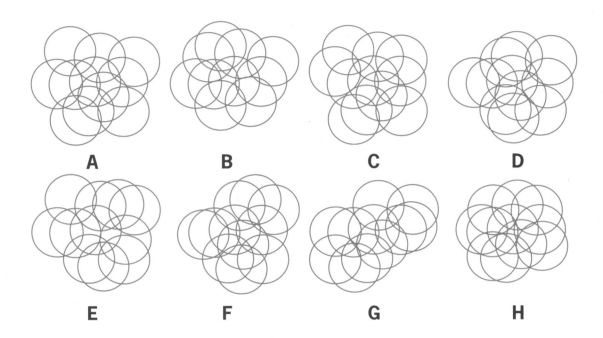

A B C D

E F G H

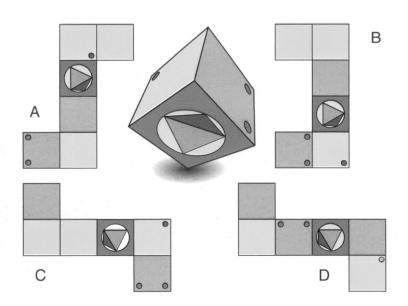

A

B

C

D

PUZZLE 422

Which of the unfolded shapes is the box in the middle opened out?

Answer see page 255

Hard
Answers

Answer 237

Answer 238
212 blocks (each set has 53).

Answer 239
A & F.

Answer 240
B. This is a mirror-image of the other shapes.

Answer 241
A.

Answer 242
D. The star is on the wrong side in relation to the other shapes.

Answer 243
C. The penguin's bill is slightly more open.

Answer 244
E. Fire is extinguised by a fire extinguisher as dirt is removed by a vacuum cleaner.

Answer 245
B. The balls on the diamond have switched places.

Answer 246
14 spotted tiles.

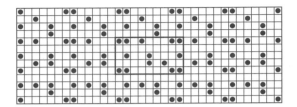

Answer 247
It will fall.

Answer 248
B and C.

Answer 249
B. Billy's plot has the greatest perimeter.

Answer 250
A & B, C & D.

Answer 251
B. It is a mirror image of the others.

Answer 252

Answer 253
Here is proof that it can be done.

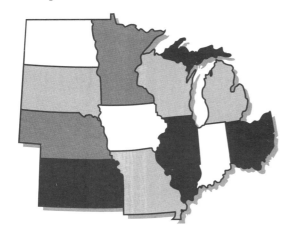

Answer 254
A. The cog and star at the bottom have changed place.

Answer 255
C. It is a mirror image.

Answer 256
157 bricks.

Answer 257
D. The others all go clockwise.

Answer 258
C.

Answer 259
H.

Answer 260
C. The lightning bolt and pointer shape have changed place at the bottom.

Answer 261
E. The white middle of the black flower in this set (top right) is larger than the others.

Answer 262
E.

Answer 263
D.

Answer 264
A.

Answer 265
The differences are:

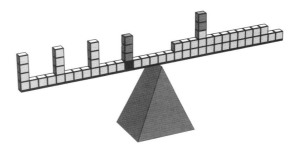

Answer 266
C and E. They are mirror images. The others are the same shape in different rotations.

Answer 267

Answer 268
B. Some of the black diamonds have moved.

Answer 269
The third on the second column and the fifth on the third column.

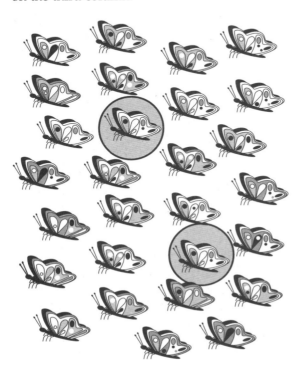

Answer 270
H. The black columns of stars move to the right, as a pair, one column at a time; when a black column reaches the right edge, it returns to the left edge in the next set.

Answer 271
31 kangaroos.

Answer 272
D. The shape is turned on its right side and the shading is reversed.

Answer 273
A and E. B, C and D are rotated images of each other.

Answer 274
D.

Answer 275
B. The separate shaded cell is always one cell away from the group of three, and, if a corner group, is on the same vertical or horizontal line as the innermost cell of the group of three.

Answer 276
It will rise.

Answer 277
42. The colors are worth Yellow 2, Green 4, Orange 6, Pink 8. The halves of each square are added together.

Answer 278
116. The colors are worth Yellow 8, Green 6, Orange 3, Pink 2. The halves of each square are multiplied.

Answer 279
14. The numbers are added. In a Pink square 5 is added, in a Green one 5 is subtracted.

Answer 280
56. Multiply top numbers and subtract sum of bottom numbers. In an Orange square subtract 4, in a Yellow one add 6.

Answer 281
(a). They will reach the ground together (although they will be much further apart). As soon as the projectile is fired it is subject to gravity, and will approach the ground at the same downward speed as the brick, despite its forward motion.

Answer 282
B. The purple balls are mirror-reversed.

Answer 283
They will move apart.

Answer 284
B. This is a mirror-image of the others.

Answer 285
D. The tick is gray.

Answer 286

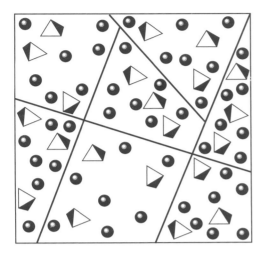

Answer 287

C. The same seven objects are repeated continuously in each line, regardless of tone.

Answer 288

A & F, B & C, D & E.

Answer 289

A.

Answer 290

The 8 crossroads are marked

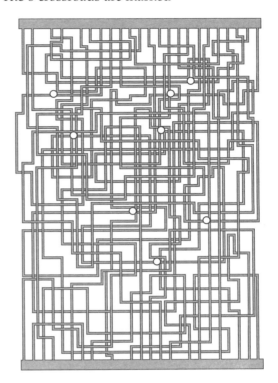

Answer 291

The missing symbol is G, the empty truck (worth 0).

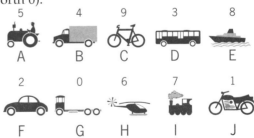

The values and working are as follows:

		4	9	5	3	1	
	×	2	8	6	7	0	
	3	4	6	7	1	7	0
	2	9	7	1	8	6	
3	9	6	2	4	8		
9	9	0	6	2			
1	4	2	0	0	5	3	7	7	0

Answer 292
C. The rectangle has moved diagonally.

Answer 293
E. The shapes rotate 72° clockwise each time.

Answer 294
F. The analogy is for two items to turn 180°, without shifting their position within the set.

Answer 295
A.

Answer 296
A and J. The loops have been distorted with respect to the others.

Answer 297
It will rise.

Answer 298
A. This is a rotated mirror-image of the other shapes.

Answer 299
13. Dove = 2; football = 3; earth = 5; spiral = 4.

Answer 300
C. Various blocks have been displaced in relation to the other shapes.

Answer 301
D. The inner shapes rotate counterclockwise; the outer shapes rotate clockwise.

Answer 302
F. All the others have one or more difference.

Answer 303
C. The figure flips onto its right side.

Answer 304
D.

Answer 305
A. In all the others there are two pairs of two objects that touch each other.

Answer 306

Answer 307
B. The spots rotate clockwise one-fifth of a turn (72°) each time.

Answer 308
B. The sequence always adds two double-curved lines onto the end of the previous pattern, at the end of the last new point added.

Answer 309

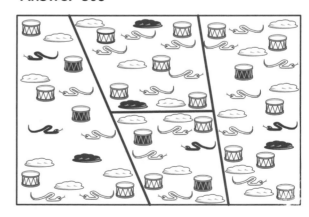

Answer 310
E. The values are:
bear = 5,
horse = 1,
fish = 4,
bird = 3.
The sums are:
5 + 1 + 1 [7] = 4 + 3 [7];
3 + 3 [6] = 5 + 1 [6];
(4 − 1) [3] + 1 [4] = 3 + 1 [4].
The column is 4 + 5 + 3
[12 or fish + fish + fish].

Answer 311
17 rattlesnakes can be collected if you follow this route:

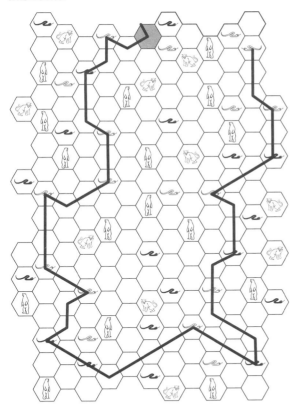

Answer 312
F. The figure has no eyebrows.

Answer 313
Follow this string:

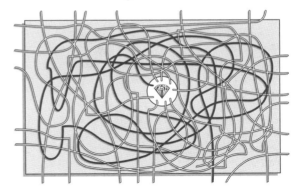

Answer 314
C. All the others have in the middle, an enlarged version of the objects at top-left and bottom-right.

Answer 315
C. Any cross in the middle three vertical tiles is always in the middle column, and the blue spot is always in the same vertical column as in the tiles to the left and right of it.

Answer 316
D. The others are all rotated versions of the same figure on the top half, with the mirror-images on the bottom half, but the mirror-image of D is on top.

Answer 317
B. The pattern rotates two sunrays one step at a time.

Answer 318
A. The balls move alternately.

Answer 319
B. All the others have the same inner and outer shape.

Answer 320
D. One of the balls has been displaced relative to the other sets, which are all rotated versions of the same set.

Answer 321
25. Multiply the numbers in opposing corners and add the products together. In a Yellow square add 7, in a Purple one subtract 9.

Answer 322
CF. In an Orange square add 5, in a Blue one add 6.

Answer 323
GF and CH. Multiply the left numbers and add to the products of the right numbers. In a Green square add 6, in an Purple one subtract 2.

Answer 324
89 (based on alphanumeric values added).

Answer 325
C. The series of five foods always retains the same order: apple, grapefruit, garlic, chicken, grape.

Answer 326
B. This is a mirror-image of the other shapes, which are all rotated versions of the same object.

Answer 327
C. The pattern is made from continuously repeating the top row of tiles, rolling over two tiles with each row.

Answer 328
C.

Answer 329
A.

Answer 330
B. The pattern rolls to the left one step at a time.

Answer 331
Both will fall.

Answer 332
B. The two sun symbols have reversed positions.

Answer 333

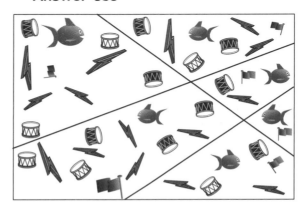

Answer 334
The helicopter (worth 2).

The symbols have the following values:

$$\div\ 7\ \begin{array}{|cccccc} 6 & 2 & 5 & 9 & 1 & 2 \\ \hline 8 & 9 & 4 & 1 & 6 \end{array}$$

$$\div\ 7\ \begin{array}{|ccccc} 8 & 3 & 4 & 4 & 0 \\ \hline 1 & 1 & 9 & 2 & 0 \end{array}$$

3 6	2 0	1 2
− 3	− 8	− 2
3 3	1 2	1 0

Answer 335
D. Starting from the left in each row, the object rolls onto its right side with each move.

Answer 336
A will rise, B will fall.

Answer 337
C. When the black arrows point down, the sequence begins with a black arrow.

Answer 338
C. The pattern rotates counterclockwise, one-tenth of a turn (36°) each step.

Answer 339
A. The analogous pattern is simply upside down.

Answer 340
B. There are 3 changes.

Answer 341

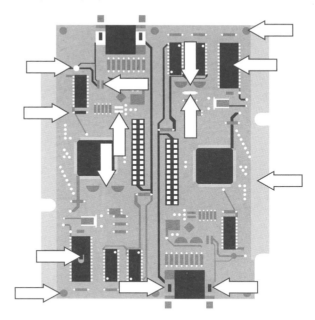

Answer 342
B. Each object in the bottom row is a right-hand mirror-image of the shape above so, in this case, the image will be the same as the object.

Answer 343
Follow the black route.

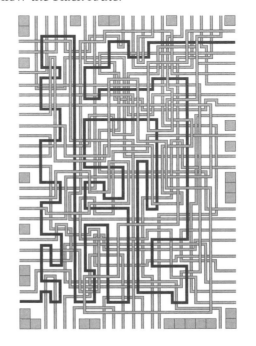

Answer 344

C.

Answer 345

F. In all others the small ball is diagonally opposite to the two shaded spikes.

Answer 346

The symbol is based on the number of shapes it appears in. For instance, the cone (bottom right) appears in two shapes, and the tube is in three.

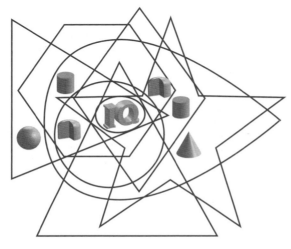

Answer 347

C.

Answer 348

A. The lightning bolt flips upside down and changes side, as in the analogous figure.

Answer 349

C. The internal configuration has changed hand in this shape.

Answer 350

Both will rise.

Answer 351

B.

Answer 352

H. The inner squares have swapped shading; the bottom row is the top row taken as a whole and flipped upside down.

Answer 353

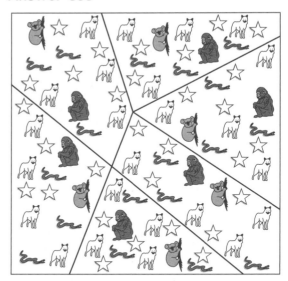

Answer 354

B. There is a block missing.

Answer 355

A. The sequence is built according to the number of enclosed spaces in each shape.

Answer 356

C. The larger shape is condensed, the whole figure is horizontally and vertically flipped and the shading changes, respectively, from black to white, white to shaded, shaded to black and black/white to white/black.

Answer 357

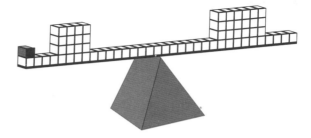

Answer 358

D. The bottom pink spot has changed place with the green spot now on its left.

Answer 359

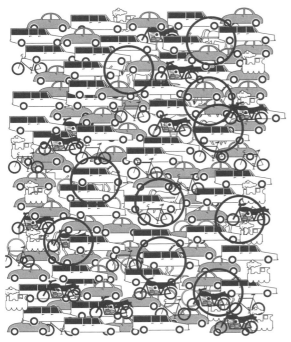

Answer 360
C. The tree has an extra inner shape.

Answer 361
B. The objects are rotating one-sixth of a turn clockwise (60°) each step.

Answer 362
B.

Answer 363
A will rise, B will drop.

Answer 364
B.

Answer 365
350 (based on alphanumeric values added).

Answer 366
61. The colors are worth Purple 3, Green 5, Red 7, Orange 9. In the top row the colors are added, in the second row they are subtracted, in the third they are multiplied, and in the fourth they are added.

Answer 367
49. The colors are worth Pink 3, Green 5, Orange 12, Yellow 15. In the tope row the colors are added, in the second they are divided, in the third they aresubtracted, and in the fourth they are multiplied.

Answer 368
5. Red is worth 3 and Green is worth 3. In the first triangle the colors are added, in the second multiplied, in the third red is added to green and blue is subtracted.

Answer 369
C. The inner shapes rotate anti- (counter) clockwise; the outer shapes rotate clockwise.

Answer 370
A.

Answer 371
D. The shape rotates one-eighth of a turn (45°) each time, but the leftmost star should be stacked below the one diagonally down to the right.

Answer 372
B and F.

Answer 373

Answer 374
D.

Answer 375

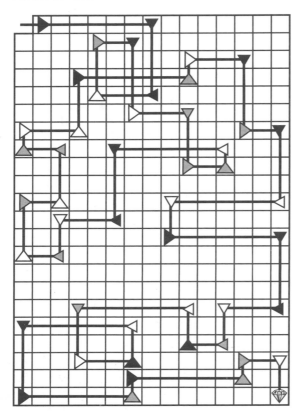

Answer 376
The lightning bolt and the drum rotate an equal amount clockwise and counterclockwise. The next drums are A, C and F.

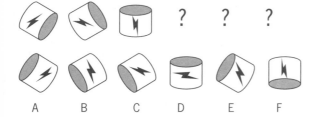

A   B   C   D   E   F

Answer 377
D. A black spot has changed position in the third row up.

Answer 378
C.

Answer 379
B. The sequence of arrows rotates counter-clockwise, and the diamond shape in the middle is the same shading as the arrow at the top.

Answer 380
D. The black vertical stripes move one column to the right one stripe each time, rolling over as it reaches the end of the shape. The black horizontal stripe moves down one row each time.

Answer 381
39 cobras.

Answer 382

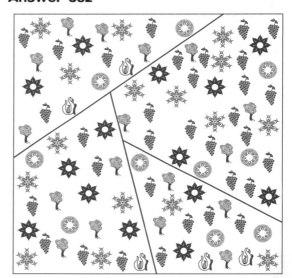

Answer 383
D. The others are 90° rotations of the same pattern.

Answer 384
G. The line shown in black is missing.

Answer 385
B and F. In all others, the yellow circle is inside the smallest outer shape.

Answer 386
A does not move, B will drop.

Answer 387
A. The values are:
leopard = 2;
flea = 3;
dog = 5;
rabbit = 4.

Answer 388
D. Not all the shapes intersect.

Answer 389

Answer 390
B. The set is turned onto its left side and reflected horizontally.

Answer 391
E. The objects are rotating around the pole in a clockwise direction; the arrow must move next to make room for the cross to come around.

Answer 392
Follow the black route.

Answer 393
C and H. Both have one more orange spot and one less purple spot.

Answer 394
D. In the other sets the single green spot is in the reflection of the point of intersection of the two black lines.

Answer 395
A, If the rows were numbered down, the sequence would be 123, 312, 231.

Answer 396
D.

Answer 397
B.

Answer 398
B. The object flips onto its left side.

Answer 399
C.

Answer 400
C. The angle between the hands remains the same, but in C the minute and hour hands are reversed.

Answer 401
B.

Answer 402
E. The jet fighter is rolling to the left one-fifth of a turn per step.

Answer 403
C.

Answer 404
D.

Answer 405
C. This is a rotated mirror-image of the others.

Answer 406

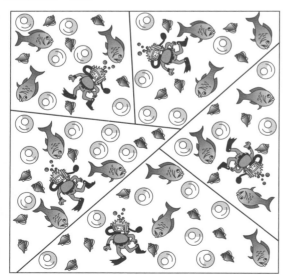

Answer 407
C. It is not a rotation of the others.

Answer 408
D and G. The line in black is missing from both.

Answer 409
3. Blue is worth 2 and Orange is 7. In the first triangle all the numbers are doubled and added, in the second they are multiplied, in the third they are added.

Answer 410
79. Green is worth 2, Red 3, Yellow 4, Blue 5, Orange 6. The halves of each square are added.

Answer 411
5. Yellow is worth 7, Orange 6, Green 5, Red 4, Blue 3. Subtract the bottom half of each box from the top.

Answer 412
256. Blue is worth 7, Yellow 6, Red 5, Green 4, Orange 3. The numbers in each square are multiplied.

Answer 413
A.

Answer 414
A. At the end of the first ramp the ball will be moving vertically, and so will fall back down, eventually coming to rest at the lowest point.

Answer 415
A will fall, B will move to the left.

MENSA MENSA MENSA MENSA MENSA MENSA MENSA MENSA

Answer 416
C. Each two halves of the analogy, when put together, make a complete 5 x 5 square.

Answer 417
B. The second figure is a rotated mirror-image of the first, and so the missing figure is a similarly rotated mirror-image of the third figure.

Answer 418
D. The arrow has come to the front of the objects below it.

Answer 419
C. The bicycle (worth 0) is missing.

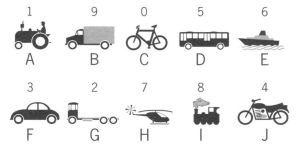

The values and working are as follows:

	1	2	6	9	3	4	25
	3	4	5	7	2	1	22
	5	7	3	4	1	8	28
	4	8	2	2	3	7	26
+	2	0	1	8	6	5	22
	1	7	3	0	1	7	5	24

Answer 420

Answer 421
D. The others are 90° rotations of the same pattern.

Answer 422
D.

HARD ANSWERS HARD ANSWERS HARD ANSWERS HARD ANSWERS HARD ANSWERS HARD